D0874056

A HANDFUL OF AUTHORS

A HANDFUL OF AUTHORS

Essays on Books and Writers

BY

G. K. CHESTERTON

Edited by

DOROTHY COLLINS

SHEED AND WARD

LONDON AND NEW YORK

FIRST PUBLISHED 1953
BY SHEED AND WARD LTD.
110/111 FLEET STREET
LONDON, E.C.4
AND
SHEED AND WARD, INC.
840 BROADWAY
NEW YORK, 3

PRINTED IN GREAT BRITAIN
BY PURNELL AND SONS, LTD.
PAULTON (SOMERSET) AND LONDON

CONTENTS

With source and dates of essays

Contents

Contents

ROBERT LOUIS STEVENSON

I

WHEN Robert Louis Stevenson was a little boy, he once made the following remark to his mother: " Mother, I've drawed a man. Shall I draw his soul now ? " This remark bears some traces perhaps of that over-formalised Scottish religion in which a man's soul was not so much himself as a very delicate younger brother whom he had to save at all costs.

But the remark has, nevertheless, a great deal of cogency in the question of all biographies, and especially in the biography of a man like Stevenson. Even if Mr. Graham Balfour's *Life* be the best ever written of one man by another, we cannot escape from the reflection of how strange it is to call such a thing a man's life. A man's life is held to mean what he did, the whole external pantomime of his existence. But this is in fact the most lifeless part of him, being the furthest removed from the centre of life. No one can know what Stevenson's life was, except, perhaps, Stevenson, who no doubt had glimmerings from time to time. The only biography that is really possible is autobiography. To recount the actions of another man is not biography, it is zoology, the noting down of the habits of a new and outlandish animal. It is most valuable and interesting, but it does not deal with the spring and spirit of a man's existence. It may fill ten volumes with anecdotes without once touching upon his life. It has drawed a man, but it has not drawed his soul. Such a statement, for example, as the statement that Stevenson was a " faddling hedonist" ought to have aroused any friend of Stevenson to an access of the most creditable bad temper.

Let us consider for a moment what were the facts. A certain human being, no matter who, was so heavily stricken with the deadly danger of the lungs that he had to lie in bed day and night, and was permitted neither to move nor to speak. On the top of this his right arm was put into a sling to prevent haemorrhage. When the joys of this condition were but half exhausted, it was discovered that his eyesight was endangered by ophthalmia from the dust, and he was consequently condemned in addition to lie in complete darkness. In this state of things his "faddling hedonism" led him to compose the greater part of *The Child's Garden of Verses*. Out of that horrible darkness and silence and immobility comes a voice that says:

> The world is so full of a number of things
> I am sure we should all be as happy as kings.

To read of such a thing is like hearing a corpse speak suddenly of birds and sunshine. It is the sublimest testimony to creation that the Creator himself could ask; the testimony of one who had lost all. Let anyone who thinks little of it smash his own lungs, disable his own arm, gag his own mouth, blind his own eyes, and then resign himself with self-indulgent gaiety to being a faddling hedonist. Is it possible that even the sevenfold stupidity of the critical spirit does not see that gaiety was valuable to Stevenson precisely because it is the most difficult of all the virtues? As most men have triumphantly maintained a level of sobriety, he triumphantly maintained a level of exhilaration. He discovered the new asceticism of cheerfulness, which will prove a hundred times harder than the old asceticism of despair. It is an idle thing, comparatively speaking, to remind the world that, gay as Stevenson was, he was only a Puritan in fancy dress. It is futile to say that, although he was hilarious, he was serious. For, as a matter of fact, no man can be merry unless he is serious. Happiness is as grave and practical as sorrow, if not more so. We might as well imagine that a man could carve a cardboard chicken or live on imitation loaves of bread, as suppose that any man could get happiness out of things that are merely light or laughable. The really frivolous man, not unknown in fashionable circles, is the man who is too frivolous to enjoy himself. Stevenson's enormous capacity for joy flowed directly out of his profoundly religious temperament. He conceived himself as an unimportant guest at one eternal and uproarious banquet, and, instead of grumbling at the soup, he accepted it with that careless gratitude which marks the baby and the real man of the world. He rode on the great galloping gift-horse of existence with the joy of a horseman at once dexterous and reckless, and did not, like so many more ambitious philosophers, nearly fall off in his desperate efforts to look the gift-horse in the mouth.

His gaiety was neither the gaiety of the Pagan nor the gaiety of the *bon vivant*. It was the greater gaiety of the mystic. He could enjoy trifles, because to him there was no such thing as a trifle. He was a child who respected his dolls because they were the images of the image of God; portraits at only two removes. He was a boy who thought his fireworks were as splendid as the stars, but it was only because he thought the stars were as youthful and as festive as the fireworks.

Very few people, however, quite understand the nature of Stevenson's play. Nothing can be more ridiculous, for example, than the solemn way in which a great many people treat Stevenson's characteristic and insane excursus into wood engraving. They gravely discuss the artistic qualities of those preposterous designs, and almost would appear to hint that Stevenson had a vocation for pictorial art. The whole thing is an admirable example of the fact that those understand Stevenson best who take him most lightly. The sole and sufficient reason why Stevenson did wood engraving was because he couldn't. It was to him simply a new game, and the pride with which he explained that he had turned an accidental scratch on the block to " a sacred ibis in the distance " was a pride in just the same blundering and foolish skill as that of a clown who tries to jump on a donkey and falls on the other side. The traces of the same mistake may be found in many observations about Stevenson's efforts in music, of which to the day of his death he knew absolutely nothing.

Stevenson's experiments in these things arose from a splendid scorn for that most false and contemptible of maxims, the statement that if a thing is worth doing, it is worth doing well. Stevenson was one of the few modern philosophers who realised the essential truth that a thing is good in its quality and not only in its perfection. If music and wood engraving are really good things they must be good even to the disciple and the fool. If an invention is marvellous and beneficent, it must be worth beholding even partially and through a glass darkly.

Doubtless it is difficult and hazardous to dogmatize about a man like Stevenson, and one estimate of his character may well be as true as the opposing one. In the honest study of a human soul we have to fling behind us such idle fictions as the notion that a thing cannot at the same time be black and white. But when every allowance has been made, I fancy that the best test of whether we understand Stevenson would be the test of whether we understand a man spending uproarious and triumphant evenings in the practise of a trade of which he knew well that he would never gain the rudiments in an eternity of lives.

Stevenson is a peculiarly difficult man for any biographer to estimate fairly. The reason lies in the fact that his personality was, as it were, singularly light and slippery, and that this slipperiness and levity arose not from eccentricity, but from a swift and unconquerable common sense. We are so rooted in open and systematic morbidities, in inhuman prejudices, in respectable monomanias, that a sane man terrifies us all like a lunatic. To us sense seems as illusive as imagination; intellectual temperance seems something wilder than excess. Stevenson was peculiarly an embodiment of this elvish sanity. He is continually startling us in his letters, not because his remarks are peculiar, but because they are a little more sensible than anything we had ever thought of. He was a sincere moralist and a sincere artist, but neither the old morality of light and darkness nor the new morality of light and shade could capture or contain him. He danced beyond them all with that divine frivolity which is the best definition of faith.

It is said in some quarters that Stevenson has been overpraised, that a reaction has set in against him, that he will not fascinate the next generation. It matters not one rap whether he does or not to anyone who has perceived his absolute solidity and his eternal use to mankind. If we in this age had a little more faith in certainties and a little less dread of caprice and reaction and changes of public opinion, we should gain more credit for sense in the long run. To the childish spirit of modern pessimism every defeat is the end of the world, every scudding cloud is the twilight of the gods. In literature, above all things, we must resist this inane panic. Stevenson will win, not because he has friends or admirers or the approval of the public or the assent of the æsthetes. He will win because he is *right*—a word of great practical import which needs to be rediscovered. He may or may not be eclipsed for a time; it would be a truer way of putting it to say that the public may or may not be eclipsed for a time. But the idea that a great literary man who has said something novel and important to mankind can vanish suddenly and finally is ridiculous. The pessimists who believe it are people who could believe that the sun is destroyed for ever every time it sinks in the west. Nothing is lost in the magnificent economy of existence; the sun returns, the flowers return, the literary fashions return. If life is a continual parting it is also a continual heaven of reconciliation. The old legends were right when they said that Arthur would come back. All things return; the world uses all its forces, the return of the stars, the return of the seasons, the return of the heroes.

II

A complete edition of Stevenson is a valuable possession for a reason which may not appear on the surface. Stevenson's method is exactly of that kind that could easily be mistaken for the mere finnicking polish of the finished artist. But he was not a mere finished artist. No mere finished artist attaches to him lovers so ardent or champions so military as Stevenson does. When ordinary men have to do with the finished artist they commonly confine themselves to wishing that he were a finished artist in another sense of the word. But Stevenson's artistic style (especially in two or three of his most celebrated books) was exactly such a performance of picked words and deliberate phrases which might easily be mistaken for a performance of dexterity and literary juggling. A strong example of this almost excessive tact and technique may be found in the tone and landscape of each of his stories. We often speak metaphorically of the colour of a narrative. In the case of Stevenson we can speak of the colour of a narrative, and use the word colour quite literally, as of the colours in a paint-box.

Each of his stories is a picture which could actually be painted in oils or water-colours, and in which there would scarcely be a jarring tint. *The Master of Ballantrae* is literally a sketch in black and white. I cannot at this moment remember a strong colour in the story; I cannot remember anyone who had red hair or anyone who habitually wore bright vesture. Dominating all is the dark figure of the Master, who always went clad in splendid black from head to foot, save for the white of his powder and the white of his ruffles. His plain brother was in complexion as dark as he. Mackellar one always conceives as dressed in dim clothes, with somewhat colourless hair. The tragedy falls mainly amid snow or storm; it is as Stevenson called it in a suggestive sub-title, " A Winter's Tale ". The main events stand against a background of grey rocks, of grey and rainy sea, or of shrubbery, which looks as grey as they do in the grey starlight of winter. The same is true of all Stevenson's most typical stories; *Treasure Island* can at once be recognised as being picked out in the brighter colours of a boy's toy theatre. Squire Livesey's face is a strong salt red; one can see it against the bright bitter green of the sea. This small matter of strictly visual colour will serve for all the other examples of this quality in Stevenson that seemed like an excess of artistic caution. He furnished his tale as if it were an artistic flat. He matched the hair of his heroine with the landscape as if he were buying her a bonnet. He made sure that the hat of the hero harmonised with the breeches of the villain. When a man does this in his two or three most celebrated books I repeat that people cannot be blamed if they get the impression that he is a mere finished technician; they cannot be blamed very much if they feel inclined to finish him with an axe.

Nevertheless, this is all a huge slander on Stevenson, and that it is a huge slander can be proved. It can be proved, that is to say, by insisting on having the whole of Stevenson and reading him *en bloc*. We should not learn his real greatness from his quality. We can only learn his real greatness from his quantity. For this exuberance and variety of work, this readiness of the man to turn his hand to anything, this vitality in so many violent experiments, all this is exactly the kind of thing that mere finicking æsthetes never do exhibit. Mere finicking æsthetes have neither the courage to do unfamiliar things nor the humility to try to do them well. One who merely worships manner apart from matter will certainly adhere to the manner that he happens to understand and to find successful. If we have all Stevenson's work before us we appreciate far better the real dimensions of his human energy and the scope of his human ambition. The man who wrote *The Master of Ballantrae* might possibly have been a mere artistic craftsman with a very congenial theme. But the man who wrote *The Master of Ballantrae* and also *The Wrong Box* must have been something greater than an artist. The man who succeeded with *Treasure Island* might be a mere stylist, but the man who succeeded with *Treasure Island* and also failed with *The Wrecker* must have been a great man.

Stevenson did not like the grotesque story of *The Body Snatcher*, but I think Stevensonians do. As in the case of all great writers, there is not one book of his that does not contain more than it seems to contain. The strongest example, perhaps, is *The Wrecker*. It is the only one of his novels that is not quite artistic in structure, and it is exactly the one of them that can be opened anywhere and read over and over again like a book of Dickens.

Robert Louis Stevenson

The real enduring quality about Stevenson even as a stylist is that there is something militant about his style; he holds the pen decisively as a man holds a sword. The quietest of his phrases has a ring of steel in it, a sound of finality. Walter Pater may be writing in good style when he tells us to burn with a hard gem-like flame. But there is something quite simple and sudden when Stevenson tells us so to live that our entrance to a room shall be like another candle being lighted. The precision of his choice of words is a deadly precision like the precision of dogma. He may be aiming very carefully, but he is aiming with a gun. The sighting may take long, but not the explosion. And this is the point of sympathy between his style and his spirit; for it was his whole business to preach that we can only have peace in this world if we accept it as a world of war.

MARK TWAIN

WE ARE always told that there is something specially sinister in the death of a great jester. I am not so sure about the point myself, seeing that so many thousand human beings, diplomatists, financiers, kings, bankers, and founders of philosophies, are engaged in functions far more ultimately fruitless and frivolous than really making the smallest schoolboy laugh. If the death of a clown makes pantomimes for a moment tragic, it is also true that the death of a statesman makes statesmanship for a moment highly comic; the irony cuts both ways. But in the case of Mark Twain there is a particular cause which at once emphasises and complicates this contrast between the comic and the serious. The point I mean is this: that while Mark Twain's literary merits were very much of the uproarious and topsy-turvy kind, his personal merits were very much of the stoical or even puritanical kind. While irresponsibility was the energy in his writings, an almost excessive responsibility was the energy in his character. The artistic European might feel that he was, perhaps, too comic when he was comic; but such a European would also feel that he was too serious when he was serious.

The wit of Mark Twain was avowedly and utterly of the extravagant order. It had that quality of mad logic carried further and further into the void, a quality in which many strange civilizations are at one. It is a system of extremes, and all extremes meet in it; thus houses piled one on top of the other is the ideal of a flat in New York and of a pagoda in Pekin. Mark Twain was a master of this mad lucidity. He was a wit rather than a humorist; but I do not mean by this (as so many modern people will certainly fancy) that he was something less than a humorist. Possibly, I think, he was something more than a humorist. Humour, a subtle relish for the small incongruities of society, is a thing that exists in many somewhat low society types, in many snobs and in some sneaks. Like the sense of music, it is exquisite and ethereal; but, like the sense of music, it can exist (somehow or other) in utter blackguards or even in utter blockheads; just as one often meets a fool who can really play the fiddle, so one often meets a fool who can really play the fool. But wit is a more manly exercise than fiddling or fooling; wit requires an intellectual athleticism, because it is akin to logic. A wit must have something of the same running, working, and staying power as a mathematician or a metaphysician. Moreover, wit is a fighting thing and a working thing. A man may enjoy humour all by himself; he may see a joke when no one else sees it; he may see the point and avoid it. But wit is a sword; it is meant to make people feel the point as well as see it. All honest people saw the point of Mark Twain's wit. Not a few dishonest people felt it.

But though it was wit it was wild wit, as wild as the pagoda in China or the other pagodas in New York. It was progressive, and the joke went forward by arithmetical progression. In all those excruciating tales of his, which in our youth made us ill with laughing, the idea always consisted in carrying some small fact or notion to more and more frantic lengths of deduction. If a man's hat was as high as a house Mark Twain would think of some way of calling it twenty times higher than a house. If his hat was smashed as flat as a pancake, Mark Twain would invent some startling and happy metaphor to prove that it was smashed twenty times flatter than a pancake. His splendid explosive little stories, such as that which describes how he edited an agricultural paper, or that which explains how he tried to decipher a letter from Horace Greeley, have one tremendous essential of great art. I mean that the excitement mounts up perpetually; the stories grow more and more comic, as a tragedy should grow more and more tragic. The rack, tragic or comic, stretches a man until something breaks inside him. In tragedy it is his heart, or, perhaps, his stiff neck. In farce I do not quite know what it is—perhaps his funny-bone is dislocated; perhaps his skull is slightly cracked.

Anyhow, the humour or wit of Mark Twain was of this ascending and exaggerative order. As such it was truly mountainous, and almost apocalyptic. No writer of modern English, perhaps, has had such a genius for making the cow jump over the moon; that is, for lifting the heaviest and most solemn absurdity high up into the most starry adventures. He was never at a loss for a simile or a parable, and they were never, strictly speaking, nonsense. They were rather a kind of incredible sense. They were not suddenly inconsequent, like Lewis Carroll; rather they were unbearably consequent, and seemed capable of producing new consequences for ever. Even that fantastic irreverence and fantastic ignorance which sometimes marked his dealings with elements he insufficiently understood, were never abrupt departures, but only elaborate deductions from his idea. It was quite logical that when told that a saint's heart had burst his ribs he should ask what the saint had had for dinner. It was quite logical that his delightful musician, when asked to play music appropriate to the Prodigal Son, should play, "We all get blind drunk when Johnny comes marching home." These are things of real wit, like that of Voltaire; though they are not uttered with the old French restraint, but with a new American extravagance. Voltaire is to them as the Rhône is to Niagara; not inferior in quality, but merely in quantity, for Niagara is not only one of the violences, but almost one of the vulgarities of Nature. The laughter of Mark Twain was like Niagara.

Such was Mark Twain; such was not Samuel Clemens. His lonely figure stands up in strange solitude and severity against the confusion and extravagance of the background of his works. The virtues which we have all now to regret in their return to God were specially virtues rather of the restrained than of the riotous or sympathetic order. We know, indeed, that he rose from the ranks, in the sense that he was poor and pugnacious in a rich and pugnacious society; that he came of Southern folk, served with the heroic Southern armies, but that the greater part of his life was such a scramble of incalculable successes and unavoidable failures as Stevenson has well described in the one convincing picture of a good American, Jim Pinkerton, in *The Wrecker*. The words Stevenson used of Pinkerton might quite truly be used of Clemens. "He was stuffed full of manly virtues. Thrift and courage glowed in him." When his hair was white and his soul heavy with years an accident led him into liabilities which the law would have discharged by the ordinary arrangements of bankruptcy. The old man refused to accept the ordinary arrangements which the law allowed him. He set to work strenuously, writing and lecturing as if he were at the beginning of his life rather than at the end of it. He repaid his unrecognised and unlegal debt, and a little later he died. Thus the primary paradox is emphasised almost in the article of death; the man whom ten million people had adored as a tom-fool was too serious even for the expectation of his own creditors.

The credit of such glowing thrift and courage (to quote an admirable phrase again) must be ascribed to something or somebody; I will no longer disguise the dreadful fact that I ascribe it exactly where Mark Twain would have ascribed it. I ascribe it to the Republican virtue of America. Of course, if

Mark Twain had said that in so many words, everybody in England would have thought he was making one of his best jokes ; whereas, in truth, he would have been indulging in one of his worst pieces of seriousness. Somebody in an advanced Socialist paper that I saw the other day said that Mark Twain was a cynic. I suppose there never was a person so far removed from cynicism as Mark Twain. A cynic must at least mean a man who is flippant about serious things ; about things that he thinks serious. Mark Twain was always serious to the verge of madness. He was not serious about St. Francis ; he did not think St. Francis serious. He honestly supposed the marvels of St. Francis to be some ecclesiastical trick of Popes and Cardinals. He did not happen to know that the Franciscan movement was something much more certainly popular than the revolution that rent America from England. He derided King Arthur's Court as something barbaric. He did not happen to know that the only reason why that dim and highly dubious Court has made a half-entry into history is that it stood, if it ever stood at all, for the remnant of high civilization against the base advance of barbarism. He did not happen to know that, in his time, St. Francis stood for the ballot-box. He did not happen to know that, in his time, King Arthur stood for the telephone. He could never quite get rid of the American idea that good sense and good government had begun quite a little while ago ; and that the heavier a monumental stone was to lift the more lightly it might be thrown away. But all these limitations of his only re-emphasise the ultimate fact : he never laughed at a thing unless he thought it laughable. He was an American ; that is, an unfathomably solemn man. Now all this is due to a definite thing, an historical thing, called Republican virtue. It was worth while to issue the Declaration of Independence if only that Mark Twain might declare his independence also.

Mark Twain

In this the great humorist not only represents his country, but a big mistake about his country. The apparent clamour and complexity of America is very superficial; America is not really advanced or aggressively civilized. New York, Philadelphia, Chicago are jokes; just such tall jokes as Mark Twain would have made. American commerce is all one tall story; American commerce is a vast American lie. But the American lie is a very serious, separate, and authoritative institution, which could only exist among a singularly truthful people. Behind these extravagances, whether in words or wealth, whether in books or bricks, there remains a grave simplicity which is truly American. The genuine value of the Yankee is not his forwardness. Rather it is his backwardness that is the real beauty of the Yankee. There is in the depths of him the rural stillness of an intellectual backwater: he is a great rustic. The log-hut, and not the sky-scraper, is the American home. Therefore, despite the revolting vices of wealth and all the vulgarities of unhistorical individualism, there does remain in the Americans a certain average of virile virtues, equality, hard work, patriotism, and a plain ideality. Corrupt fatigue is uncommon; unclean despair is almost unknown. You could not have made Mark Twain even understand either of these things. He was radiant with a rectitude none the less noble for being slightly naive; he carried everywhere those powerful platitudes that are like clubs of stone. With these he hammered Calvinism in his youth and Christian Science in his old age. But he was not an "advanced" thinker, not a mind in revolt; rather he was a conservative and rustic grandfather older than all such follies. But this strength in him and his country truly came from a great spirit which England resisted and has forgotten; the spirit which, when all is said, made it no nonsense to compare Washington to Cincinnatus; the austere love of liberty and of the ploughshare and the sword.

ON SEEING *LES QUINZE*

I TWICE had the pleasure of seeing the admirable performance of the French company " Les Quinze du Vieux Colombier ", who performed first at the Arts Theatre Club and afterwards, I think, at the Ambassadors. The pleasure was of many kinds, and not least in hearing, what I have not heard for a long time, the living and leaping beauty of the great French language, as spoken by those who know how to speak it. Like most pleasures that have that peculiar quality of swiftness, it seems at the moment difficult even to record or recall, let alone to define. The first suggestion that occurs to the mind is that all other languages move on hinges or joints, but that the French language darts and flickers like a flame. But this suggestion would be incorrect as an explanation. A flame is a fluid, in a sense; it is elemental in the sense of indivisible. But the best French speech is not only very much more than mere sound, but very much more than mere music. It is flexible, because it is not less but more articulate than what we commonly call articulate speech. It is significant that we use the word articulation in two senses; we talk of the articulation of a sentence and of the articulation of a skeleton. The French tongue is like a serpent; in that it has so many articulations as to produce the general impression of a curve. It has so many joints that it seems to have no joints at all. A man can coil a snake round and round inside his hat, though only a few individuals have indulged in this form of nature-study. If a man were to attempt to fold up a giraffe, or even to deal in this manner with the most compact or collapsible horse or dog, he would find that they were not sufficiently articulated animals. The rapid French talk is flexible in the sense of seeming to fit into every inch or corner of conversation ; because those who speak it, the heirs of the most central civilization of civilized Europe, are the most articulate of all those whom the Greek poet called "articulate-speaking men".

But the problem of folding up a giraffe so as to pack him in a hat, like the analogous problem of coaxing the camel through the eye of the needle, belongs to an order of animal fantasies which are suggested by this text in another way. The first play which I saw performed by the French players was a play about Noah and the Ark ; and necessarily consisted largely of animals. The production or stage management had very wisely made them comic and symbolic animals. In fact, they might fairly be described as heraldic animals. I remember, with a slight shudder, that there was a time when theatrical managers prided themselves on their realism. I know not whether these realists would really have brought real lions and tigers among the actors. Perhaps that would have caused too realistic a shudder even for realists. But they would be quite capable of sinking huge sums of money, and going through agonies of artificial lighting, grouping, stuffing and winding up of clockwork, with the base and degrading purpose of making the lions look like lions. The result of such bravado of realism is always the loss of reality. What was the matter with these theatrical managers was that they were such very theatrical managers. The object of their accuracy was not truth, but a triumph of deception. About the fantastic animals of the Ark there was no deception. They were facts ; as all avowed fables are facts. It struck me that there was a certain parallel between this affair of the animals and the setting of the second French play I saw in the same place ; a play about the old Roman story of Lucretia and Tarquin. The dreadful realists of the theatre, the men who spared no expense, were often particularly proud of a pedantic accuracy about historical costume. And in this case I felt that the accuracy would be very pedantic. Brutus and Collatinus or Tarquin would have been heavily attired in togas and tunic, if possible of the precise date of the first foundation of the Roman Republic. I am glad to say that in this case the producers did not bother about pedantic accuracy, or indeed about accuracy at all. They boldly set the whole scene amid the conventions of Renaissance tragedy; Tarquin might have been a rather extra paganised Caesar Borgia; while Brutus wore his hair in a way that was more reminiscent of Molière. I felt at once that it was exactly right; nay, that it was historically right. And it seemed to me that both in the case of the comic animals and the conventional costumes, there was a principle involved that has never been expressed rightly. I will therefore proceed to express it wrongly.

Shapes that have passed through the mind of man exist, in a second and special sense, which does not belong to them while they are merely in unconscious nature. There must be many minute creatures that have passed through the microscope and have not yet fully passed into the mind. If a man were to blazon a bacillus on his shield, it would not be instantly recognized, like a lion or a leopard. Yet the lion that is recognized is quite unlike the lion that is real; and the leopard on the shield is a very unscientific version of the leopard in the Zoo. If a man were to wave a flag decorated with three microbes on a chevron, it would not have the inspiring effect of the old French flag decorated with lilies, or even of the yet older Frankish flag said to have been decorated with toads. There are at least legends about toads; they had an undeserved reputation for carrying jewels in their heads; but nobody has ever started digging for diamonds in the inside of a microbe. A microbe is perhaps not a fair test, because of its small stature and shy and retiring disposition. But it would be just as true of a mammoth as of a microbe, if we really had no poetic associations or literary legends about mammoths. We hear a great deal of the huge inhuman impersonal powers of cosmos or chaos and how inspiring they are to the imagination; but they are not really very inspiring until the imagination has worked on them for some time. The mind of man is the mirror in which these shapes become shapes of doom. And if the object be an instant attack on the imagination, as it is in the case of the drama, it is strictly true to say that a thing is not even fearful unless it is familiar.

Thus the true image of the lion is that which has been made part of the image of God. It is the lion of magnanimity, the lion of royalty, the lion who will not hurt virgins, the lion who was the emblem of the humanity of Christ. It is not the large cat whom somebody shoots with a gun or shuts up in a cage. For the purpose of immediate dramatic effect, it is necessary to be conventional; because convention does really mean the meeting-place of the emotions of myriads of men. The same truth applies to tragedies like that of Tarquin; and their deliberate disguise in externals centuries later than Tarquin. These things represent not only Tarquin but the terror of Tarquin; the long shadow that his deed of shame cast down the centuries. We feel it more and not less when we hear that terrible voice in an Elizabethan echo; or see that dark figure in strange Florentine armour. As the only real lion is the lion that a child can dream of, so the only convincing Tarquin is the Tarquin who has been a nightmare to numberless dramatists and dreamers. This concerns artistic truth, of course, as distinct from scientific and historical truth; which have their own objective object. But if we are talking of the effect of symbols on the soul, it is broadly true that they are best when they are most symbolic. For in man also is something of the divine; and the things that enter his world pass through a second creation.

THE TRUE ROMANCE

THIS IS a perfectly true story; but there is in it a certain noble irony, not very easy to analyse, which goes down to the very roots of Christianity.

Some hundreds of years ago there was born in one of the southern peninsulas of Europe a man whose life was very like the life of a boy in one of Mr. Henty's books. He did everything that could possibly be expected of a boy's hero; he ran away to sea; he was trusted by admirals with important documents; he was captured by pirates; he was sold as a slave. Even then he did not forget the duties of a Henty hero. He made several picturesque and desperate attempts at escape, scaling Moorish walls and clambering through Moorish windows. He confronted the considerable probability of torture, and defied it. But he was not like the unscrupulous prison-breakers, like Cellini or Casanova, ready to break the world as well as the wall, or his promise as well as his prison. He remembered that he was the hero of an honest boy's story-book, and behaved accordingly. Long afterwards his country collected the depositions of the other Christian captives, and they were an astonishing chorus. They spoke of this man as if he were a sort of saint, of the almost unearthly unselfishness with which he divided their distresses and defied their tormentors. As one reads the coldest biographical account one can feel the alien air, that enormous outside world of Asia and Africa that has always felt slavery to be a natural and even monotonous thing. One feels the sunny silence of great open courts, with fountains in the midst, guarded here and there by mute, white-clad, unnatural men; dim and secret divans smelling of smoke and sweet stuff; grass burnt out of the bare ground, and palm trees prised like parasols. And in all this still horror of heat and sleep, the one unconquered European still leaping at every outlet of adventure or escape; climbing a wall as he might a Christian apple tree, or calling for his rights as he might in a Christian inn.

Nor did our hero miss that other great essential of the schoolboy protagonist; which is accidental and even improbable presence on a tremendous historical occasion. All who love boys' books as they should be loved know that Harry Harkaway, as well as crossing cutlasses with an individual smuggler or slaver, must also manage to be present at the Battle of Trafalgar. The young musketeer from Gascony, however engrossed by duels with masked bravos or love-letters to Marguerite de Valois, must not forget to put in an appearance at the Massacre of St. Bartholomew. Here also my hero in real life equalled any of the heroes of juvenile fiction; for he was present and took an active part in one of the most enormous and earth-changing events in history. Europe, in the age in which he lived, was, as it is now, in one of its recurring periods of division and disease. The Northern nations were full of sombre fanaticisms; the Southern nations of equally sombre statecraft and secrecy. The country of the man I describe was indeed rich in territory; but its King was morbid, mean, and lethargic; a man of stagnant mysteries, as he looks in those fishy, pasty-faced portraits which still endure. His strong but sinister imperial armies were engaged in wars, more or less unjust on both sides, with the sinister enthusiasms of the North; the whole civilization was bitter and trivial, and apparently tumbling to pieces. And at this moment appeared upon its Eastern borders its ancient and awful enemy, the Turk.

Like genii summoned out of that Eastern sea by the seal of

Solomon, robed in the purple of the twilight or the green of the deep, rose the tall, strange, silent sails of the admirals of Islam. The very shapes of the ships on the horizon were unfamiliar and fearful; and when they came close to the Greek islands, prow and stern showed the featureless ornament of the foes of idolatry; that featureless ornament in which one seems to see a hundred faces, as one does in a Turkey carpet. The ships came silently and ceaselessly, in numbers that, it seemed, had never been seen since Xerxes seemed stronger than the gods. And every hermit on a Greek headland, or little garrison of knights upon an islet in the Mediterranean, looked at them and saw the sunset of Christendom.

They encircled and besieged a stronghold in that central sea, whose fall would have been the fall of Europe. In the general paralysis the Pope, with one exception, was the only man who moved promptly; he put out the Papal galleys and addressed a public prayer for help to all the Christian princes. The cold and sluggish King doubted and hung back, just as he would have done in the historical novel. But he had a half-brother—as he would have had in the novel. The half-brother was every bit as brave, handsome, brilliant, and generous as he would have been in the novel. The King was as jealous of him as he would have been in the novel. This quite genuine hero rushed to the rescue, and in such crises it is popularity that tells, even in empires. The young Prince had already won romantic victories in Africa, but he could bring only a few ships in time for the attack. Then was waged on that blue and tideless sea what must have been one of the most splendid and appalling battles that ever stained the sea or smoked to the sun. The Turks slew eight thousand Christian soldiers, and the sea drank galley after galley of the Christian fleet. But the fight was sustained with that terrible and intolerant patience that only comes in a collision of strong creeds, when one whole cosmos really crashes into the other. Before night the tide of that river of blood began to turn. Thirty thousand of the Turks were killed or taken prisoners, and out of the Turkish ports and galleys came into light and liberty twelve thousand European slaves.

This was the great battle of Lepanto, and of course our hero was there, sword in hand; of course he was wounded there. I can fancy him standing on the deck, with his arm in a sling and looking at the slender escape of Europe and the purple wreck of Asia with a sad, crooked smile on his face. For he was a person whose face was capable of expressing both pity and amusement. His name was Miguel de Cervantes Saavedra, commonly called Cervantes. And having another arm left, he went home and wrote a book called *Don Quixote*, in which he ridiculed romance and pointed out the grave improbability of people having any adventures.

THE DIVINE PARODY OF *DON QUIXOTE*

IT IS the peculiar fate of things several centuries old that they have to be treated with the most prodigious austerity, even when they are in themselves things entirely hilarious and simple. Venerable doctors of the Church spend their lives in studying ancient Roman pots and pans, the replicas of which hang up in their own kitchens, and in editing and annotating ancient Greek pantomimes which they would petition the County Council, in the name of public decency, to turn off the boards of the Tivoli.

To the merely literary mind there seems something quite as superfluous in treating *Don Quixote* as a learned matter as in so treating *The Bab Ballads* or *The Innocents Abroad*. Literature celebrates the eternal youth of humanity; in literature all men are equal, in century as well as in station. The feelings with which it deals are always fresh; in its wild empire an Englishman may fall in love with an Ancient Egyptian princess, and by its laws a man may marry his grandmother. *Don Quixote* may be read by a child without preface or explanation; it tells its own story; and if there is much more in the story than most of us have ever found, that dark treasure is to be sought in the story and not in the notes.

The second part of *Don Quixote*, which is generally reckoned inferior to the first, is superior to it in many qualities of construction and verisimilitude even if it is entirely inferior in farcical episode, in burlesque force, and in the most obvious effects of humour. But I venture to question whether the superiority which Goethe and Lamb found in the first part was based merely upon that preposterous picturesqueness which lends such an everlasting vividness to the tournament of the windmills and the castle that was really an inn. The first part is probably superior because it contains more of the fire of that essential philosophy which lies at the heart of this great romance. In order fully to realise this we must make some attempt to bring before our minds the spiritual energy of which, as in all books, the story is only the product and the symbol.

The great truth which lies at the heart of *Don Quixote* is the truth that the conflict of the world is chiefly a conflict between goods. The battle between the idealism of Don Quixote and the realism of the inn-keeper is a battle so hot and ceaseless that we know that they must both be right. A vulgar philosophy laments the wickedness of the world, but when we come to think of it we realise that the confusion of life, the doubt and turmoil and bewildering responsibility of life, largely arise from the enormous amount of good in the world.

There is much to be said for everybody; there are too many points of view; too many truths that contradict each other, too many loves which hate each other. Our earth is not, as Hamlet said, "an unweeded garden", but a garden which is choked and disordered with neglected flowers. The eternal glory of *Don Quixote* in the literary world is that it holds perfectly even the two scales of the mysticism of the Knight and the rationalism of the Squire. Deep underneath all the superficial wit and palpable gaiety of the story there runs a far deeper kind of irony—an irony that is older than the world. It is the irony that tells us that we live in a maddening and perplexing world, in which we are all right; and that the battle of existence has always been like King Arthur's last battle in the mist, one in which "friend slew friend, not knowing whom he slew".

That is a sobering thought, but assuredly it is not a depressing one. Scarcely any book is more profoundly humane and steadfast than *Don Quixote*, more filled with a vast and elemental assumption that human nature is good. The threads of our life cross and tangle, but it is not we who hold the skein. The philosophy of Cervantes cries aloud to the world the much misunderstood and increasingly forgotten, but always divine and wholesome, science of minding one's own business. It stands for the great and practical paradox that the narrowest duty is also the broadest, that it is very universal to bake a cake or rock a cradle, and generally very vulgar and provincial to take charge of the universe. This great hospitality of the brain of Cervantes, this readiness to admit that lawlessness itself was only a war of a hundred justices, gives him his great place in literature.

He does not in any pre-eminent degree owe that place to his diction or his style. He owes it to the fact that this impartiality of his is the very soul of great literature, for literature should know all men and judge none. It is the dead who are judged, and the creatures of literature should never die.

An example of somewhat the same inscrutable and therefore eternal situation that is found in *Don Quixote* may be found, for instance, in the *Bacchae* of Euripides. There also we have to do with the war waged by a robust and righteous common sense with a fierce, fugitive, and unclassified religious transport. In that, also, we are left at the end doubtful which party was right, and whether the author of that dark play was writing as a pious enthusiast or as a sneering sceptic. In *Don Quixote*, however, the matter is clearer. He belongs to our own civilization, and between that civilization and the civilization of the ancient world there is a great gulf fixed. The madness of Don Quixote seems to us much less mad than the sanity of antiquity. The windy and crazy adventures which set him to smite windmills and slaughter sheep are to us less monstrous and imbecile than many of the established loves and traditions which were followed in broad daylight by sublime philosophers in the streets of sublime cities. For the core of the truth is that we have the follies of Don Quixote in our very blood; we are by irrevocable generation children of the Middle Ages. Adventure and ceremonial, chivalry and idolatry, fantastic pride and a fantastic humility lie at the very root of our institutions and in the inmost chamber of our imagination. Cervantes, with a fearless realism, led his hero almost a dance of degradation through the man-traps and cross-purposes of the coarse world, rolled him in ditches, and beat him with cudgels. But the fact remains that we all read *Don Quixote* because we are all knight-errants; we read it for the sake of Don Quixote's dream, and without that dream the whole story would be as flat and common as the chronicles of Camden Town.

Don Quixote, then, is a part of all of us, and a part which will always remain and give a great deal of trouble to any persons who wish to tie us up finally in any political constitution or synthetic philosophy. The knight figures in Cervantes' romance as the foe of that civilization which thinks that everything is best trusted to an institution. In the story he is the last individual; he has the hopeless individualism of the Irishman. If injustice is being done he cannot see that cutting down the oppressor with the sword is any less reasonable than writing to the Society for the Prevention of Cruelty to Children. To trust entirely to this hare-brained justice as a basis of our civilization would be absurd, but it will be found even more absurd in the long run to ignore it or to root it out. For the whole of our huge weight of laws and restrictions hangs in the last resort upon this single thread of visionary valour. Our whole social ideal is as daring and fanciful as Don Quixote's dream, and there is not much to choose between his tilting at the sails of the windmills and our tilting at the great wheel of the world.

W. W. JACOBS

MR. JACOBS is in a real sense a classic. When I say he is classical, I do not merely mean that he is eminently able; Mr. Rudyard Kipling (for example) is eminently able, but he has not the pure marmoreal classicism of Mr. Jacobs. Compared with Mr. Kipling, Mr. Jacobs is like the Parthenon.

He is strictly to be described as classical for this reason—that he is a return to the central and sane tradition of humorous literature. He is the child of Dickens, and he has wiped out the weary interregnum between himself and his father. We find ourselves again in a farce older than Aristophanes; and we realize that of all the iron elements in the eternal soul none is more fixed or more enduring than its frivolity. Man has remembered his ancient laughter. In the period between the end of Dickens and the appearance of Mr. Jacobs we have had a great number of really great wits and of really great humorists. We have had men like Whistler whose wit seemed almost inspired, and whose repartee came like a bolt from the blue. We have had humorists like Mr. Max Beerbohm whose humour was so dainty and delicate as to be a kind of topsy-turvy transcendentalism. But these great wits and great humorists had one genuine defect—they could not laugh. They could smile, they could sneer, they could in desperate cases chuckle; but laughter, which is an elemental agony, shaking the jester himself, was a thing outside their mode of life.

There is no necessary connexion between wit and mirth. A man's wit overpowers his enemies; but his mirth overpowers him. As long as a man is merely witty he can be quite dignified;

in other words, as long as he is witty he can be entirely solemn. But if he is mirthful he at once abandons dignity, which is another name for solemnity, which is another name for spiritual pride. A mere humorist is merely admirable; but a man laughing is laughable. He spreads the exquisite and desirable disease by which he is himself convulsed. But our recent comedians have distrusted laughter for exactly the same reason that they have distrusted religion or romantic love. A laugh is like a love affair in that it carries a man completely off his feet; a laugh is like a creed or a church in that it asks that a man should trust himself to it.

A man must sacrifice himself to the God of Laughter, who has stricken him with a sacred madness. As a woman can make a fool of a man, so a joke makes a fool of a man. And a man must love a joke more than himself, or he will not surrender his pride for it. A man must take what is called a leap in the dark, as he does when he is married or when he dies, or when he is born, or when he does almost anything else that is important.

Now there are at least four points in which Mr. Jacobs represents the return to the great comic classics; and this is the first of them—the fact that he re-establishes humour as something violent and involuntary and outside ourselves. His best humour is outside criticism, in the sense that physical pain is outside criticism. With him as with Dickens, an absurdity is an absurdity as a blow in the face is a blow in the face. You cannot pause to call the joke a bad joke. You cannot pause to call the joke a good joke. It is simply a fact of natural history that you, having read a certain remark two minutes before, are now rolling about on the carpet and waving your legs in the air.

There can be no criticism about this comic genius, because nobody in its presence can remain in a critical frame of mind.

When, let us say, Mr. Dick Swiveller is cut out by Mr. Cheggs, the market gardener, he prepares a dramatic departure, and Miss Wackles says she is very sorry. " Sorry ! " says Mr. Swiveller, " sorry in the possession of a Cheggs ! " Nobody reading those words for the first time could ever decide whether they were low comedy or high comedy, broad humour or fine humour, large, small, long, short, fat, or thin humour ; he would merely realize that they were humorous. He would be stunned by the simple fact that the thing was funny.

So it is in the best of Mr. Jacobs' work. In one of his stories, for instance, the night-watchman expresses a contempt for the pugilistic device of the punch-ball, and recalls the exploits of a more uncorrupted pugilist who was in the habit, when he wanted practice, of putting on a soft hat like a Nonconformist minister and going into a pub and contradicting people. " He'd 'ave no more thought of 'ittin' a pore 'armless ball than I should of thought of 'ittin' 'im." That kind of sentence has the same direct Dickens quality. It is an unanswerable absurdity. It is very difficult to judge it, although doubtless after some little time or in some special detachment we can judge it. But we can only judge it after we have laughed at it. In other words, we can only judge it after we have acquitted it.

The second point is this : that he re-establishes the old comic importance of the thing called plot. Many other modern humorists have written short tales that were inspirations, fancies, glimpses, ideas. He alone has written short tales that are ingenious merely as tales. Every one of Mr. Jacobs' stories is an amplified anecdote ; that is to say, it is a thing with a complication and a climax, a climax which must be at once expected and unexpected. In this matter Mr. Jacobs is entirely in line with the oldest mirth of mankind. The great classic conception of a good story is that it should have a point, and that the principal character should sit down on it. Thus, for instance, the story of Polyphemus and No-man is an enlarged anecdote. Thus the many old tales of ingenious riddles and still more ingenious answers (such as that of King John and the Abbot of Canterbury and several about Solomon and the Queen of Sheba) are all enlarged anecdotes. The fun is not merely in the characters, it is in the whole framework of the thing; it is structurally funny, architecturally funny. Here, then, we have the second of the four classical qualities of Mr. Jacobs. We have here the fact that he is greatly concerned with the argument of his epic; with the thing to be done and the outer fate that falls upon his characters. And he feels and satisfies that desire for mere funny incidents well narrated which was once satisfied in savage tents and is still satisfied in smoking-rooms.

His third agreement with the classics lies in his lucidity. His humorous style is indeed allusive; and the nature of that allusiveness I shall discuss in a moment; but it is perfectly popular and clear. Consequently he has no concern with that air of mystery in which so many able moderns have wrapped their amusement. The old jester was disappointed that men did not see the joke. The new jester is delighted that they do not see the joke. Their blank faces are a proof of his own exquisite and individualised talent; the joke is too good to be seen. Laughter has been from the beginning the one indestructible brotherhood, the one undeniably social thing. But these moderns have made even laughter a lonely thing. They are always hunting for a humour that shall be completely original. But if a thing were completely original it would be completely unintelligible. If a man made an entirely new language it would not be a language at all. Mr. Jacobs represents here again a return to the normal; to a humour that is rich but simple, to a humour that is humorous but also obvious, to a humour which is not vulgar but which is common.

But there is one point in which Mr. Jacobs touches greatness, compared with which all these others are unimportant. This is his achievement as an interpreter of a great element of the democracy. He is the artistic expression of the humour of the people; a point in which (in the phrase of the French Revolution) "the people is supreme". He exaggerates that popular humour undoubtedly. But that popular humour is itself in its nature an exaggeration; and the more exaggerated his popular humour is, the more like it is to popular humour. He over-states the actual statements of navvies or sailors; but they themselves would over-state them if they could. It would be a mistake to say that he made plebeian satire an art; but the plebeians have already made it an art. It would be truer to say that Mr. Jacobs' gibes are masterpieces where the real gibes of the street are merely works of art. Mr. Jacobs' labourers say better things than most real labourers, but the same kind of things. The first bears the same relation to the second that the rustic songs of Shakespeare bear to the rustic songs of Stratford-on-Avon.

"Take your face 'ome and bury it; not under plants as you're fond of." That might stand as a comparatively central and typical example of the tradition of satire that can actually be heard in the streets. That has all the three essential characteristics of the wit of the populace. First, it is poetical, or, at least, close to poetry; for everything that is close to the people is close to poetry. It is poetical, I mean, in the essential sense that it is connected with the ultimate enigma of nature and with wild and beautiful images. There is all the strength of a dark and grotesque lyric of Heine in the idea of the hideousness of the buried head polluting the very process of life, and distorting the very flowers and leaves. It is like the tale of the Pot of Basil. Second, the expression typifies popular humour in the fact that it is a joke about the body, about physical ugliness; a kind of joke that is an essential of moral health. To take the body seriously is to take the first step towards all the disasters that destroyed the Pagan civilization. Of all the quaint sanities which are the secrets of Christianity perhaps the sanest is the fact that it feels the body to be something grotesque. And of all forms of taking the body seriously, not one (not even the vile thing called hygiene) is so bad as the form that takes ugliness seriously as a sacred unmentionable thing. If you make a point of delicacy out of ugliness, you make a religion out of ugliness. Our moderns think it very shocking to pour any derision upon the body: they prefer to pour it upon the soul.

But the people never are and never can be moderns. That is why I am a democrat. The men in the street laugh at a man's nose which they can see, and which is often absurd, not at his religion, which they cannot see, and which is never absurd. Mr. Jacobs is the champion of the old, healthy habit of telling people how funny they look. All his conversationalists are given to being what is called "personal". I do not know anything more reasonable than being personal when you are talking about a person. But undoubtedly for the last thirty years our discussions have been growing more impersonal. There has been more airiness, detachment, and refinement in our arguments, and in consequence much more swindling in our public service.

No one can forget the almost endless list of Mr. Jacobs' popular discussions of physiognomy. There was Mr. Bob Pretty, who told his colleague, the old game-keeper, that he "'oped his face wouldn't get knocked about like that", and when the game-keeper indignantly denied that his face had been knocked about, said, with sudden meekness, "Oh! I beg your pardon. I didn't know it was natural." There was the sarcastic bar-keeper, who met his match in the more sarcastic boy, telling the youth to take the head off his beer, or he'd " muss his moustache up ". To whom the boy replied that "as long as it didn't turn 'em red he didn't mind so much". There was the meditative miller, who remarked to the farmer with inconsiderate emphasis on the mystery of where the farmer's daughter could have got her good looks from. " She's no more like you than you're like a warming-pan—not so much."

Finally, the farcical speech of Mr. Jacobs' characters is undoubtedly ingenious, and even elaborate, but in this respect more than in any other it is the real speech of the populace. The real speech of the real mob is more intricate than medieval heraldry. To anybody who has ever talked to the man in the street it must be infinitely amusing to hear the philosophers of aristocracy talking about the sort of joke the vulgar can understand. There is not one of those philosophers of aristocracy who could before an impartial tribunal hold his own for five minutes against a cabman. Mr. Jacobs is in literature the voice of the inspired cabman.

But the wit of the cabman and the populace is not merely excellent—it is even subtle. It is even too subtle. Slang is the very reverse of a coarse thing. It is, if anything, an over-complex and over-civilized thing. It has some of that systematic indirectness which makes a darkness in the late medieval philosophy and poetry. This twisted luxuriance is perfectly represented in the admirable locutions of Mr. Jacobs' angry sailors. Taking the nose, or mental capacity, or family circumstances of an enemy as a mere text or starting point, the Jacobs sailor gets out of it a sort of jungle of tropical taunts. One thing at least Mr. Jacobs has done—he has compiled the most reliable encyclopædia of insults that can be purchased in the market.

I repeat, then, that I find Mr. Jacobs a classic; that is, a return to the enduring style. Many who have enjoyed his books will think that I have here taken him too seriously. On that point I have one word to say in conclusion. I have had no space to deal adequately with his amazing tales of tragedy, such as *Jerry Bundler* or the admirable *Monkey's Paw*. But if the reader will look at them he will notice this fact: that they stand alone among our modern tales of terror in the fact that they are dignified and noble. They rise out of terror into awe. Everyone will remember the mother who wished to see the mangled nothing that was once her son. Everyone will remember that other tale of the son who sat in darkness because of his blasted face, and its final sentiment, "Here is to the children my son saved." Everyone will remember them; but it is more important that, ghastly as they are, everyone will be glad to remember them. His humour is wild, but it is sane humour. His horror is wild, but it is a sane horror. His farce is classic farce because, however violent it is, it leaves the heart more happy. And his tragedy is classic tragedy, because however heartrending it is, it leaves the heart more strong.

VICTOR HUGO

THE CENTENARY of Victor Hugo, which has just been celebrated in Paris, arouses some of the deepest thoughts which are possible in the human mind. Hugo represents the culmination of a revolution which almost in our own time shook the foundations of humanity, and already that revolution is old, and Hugo is a vague and remote figure, a doubtful and little discussed author. Yet he was, beyond question, one of the greatest men of letters that Europe has seen, and the day of his return into intellectual triumph is remote indeed, but certain. There can be little doubt that we are divided from the generations that immediately precede us by a gulf far more unfathomable than that which divides us from the darkest ages and the most distant lands. There are art-critics who maintain that the most archaic and Byzantine beginnings of Christian art are superior to everything that goes by the name of an Italian master. There are art-critics who maintain that a portion of a Persian carpet contains and eclipses everything that can be found in the National Galleries of Europe. It is, upon the whole, exceedingly probable that there are art-critics who maintain that the two idols from the Fiji Islands which used to stand outside the British Museum are artistically superior to all the Greek gods and goddesses which are to be found inside. But there is a limit to this modern liberality: there are certain forms of art which are most recent and most effective upon the minds of our immediate forbears. No one declares that the Regency style of dress, or style of poetry, or style of architecture, was the most perfect in the world. No one says that Opie was the first painter, or Flaxman the first sculptor, or George IV the first gentleman of Europe.

Victor Hugo

The time is no doubt coming when a languid and æsthetic collector will exhibit, as treasures dating from the true time of art's supremacy, the furniture and costume of the Early Victorian Era. He will boast of possessing a real case of wax flowers under glass, an authentic sampler, and a real lustre chandelier from a real Brighton landlady. But that time is not yet. For the present we are doomed to misunderstand the time which produced us. We can comprehend the most immoral outbursts of ancient Israel; but our immediate progenitors are strangers to us. We worship our remotest ancestor, but we teach our grandmother.

I have dwelt upon this particular aspect of the matter because it is supremely necessary to understand it if we wish properly to understand Victor Hugo. He represented two great revolutions, the first artistic and the second political. The artistic revolution was that connected with the word romanticism: the political revolution was that connected with the word democracy. And the great difficulty involved in properly appreciating him lies in this, that both romanticism and democracy have conquered and therefore become commonplace. They have been so triumphant as to become invisible; just as existence itself is triumphant and invisible. And like existence itself they have become truisms: and while it is fatally easy to turn a truth into a truism, it is fatally difficult to turn a truism back into a truth. We may sympathise with a dead faith, but it is difficult to sympathise with an apparently dead scepticism. In history even a molehill is more expressive than an extinct volcano. Those who may be called, with all respect, the eternal tootlers of the ages, Horace and Catullus and Villon and Tom Moore, are always sure of sympathy. But those who have blown the trumpet to a veritable charge, like Luther and Victor Hugo, are doomed to exhibit themselves to history as making a gigantic fuss about nothing.

The great achievements of Hugo are sufficiently obvious even if we consider only his novels, which are probably the most popular, though certainly not the most important of his works. Every one of his great novels was in itself a small French Revolution. In *Notre Dame de Paris* he revealed to the modern world all the beauties and terrors of the old medieval order, and showed how pitilessly the individual was sacrificed to such an order. In *Les Misérables* he showed, with a far more sensational illumination, how our own modern order of law and judgment and criminal procedure was, as far as the sacrifice of individuals was concerned, as cruel as any medieval order. In *Ninety-Three* he showed that such a sacrifice of individuals became necessary, and in a strange, bitter manner, attractive, even in the modern age. In all his works alike there are two common characteristics. The first is a tendency to what is called sensationalism ; the second is a tendency to what is called democracy. It is necessary to realise his feeling upon both these points before we do anything like justice to him.

It is the custom among certain literary men of this era to sneer at the novels of Hugo, chiefly on the ground that they are sensational ; as if all art were not sensationalism and the whole artistic temperament best definable as the temperament which is sensational or receptive of sensations. But the novels of Victor Hugo have one very actual and direct claim upon the attention of everybody. They are, in one sense, the most interesting of all novels. The reason is that Hugo is typically a mystic, a man who finds a meaning in everything. We all know what are the uninteresting, the inevitably uninteresting parts of fiction ; we all know what parts of a novel to skip. We skip the long description of the country where the hero was born, with its flat sandy wastes, made ragged with fir trees and tumbling towards the West into low discoloured hills. We skip the long account of the heroine's room, with its quaint old carved furniture and the portraits on the wall, dim with age but gorgeous with ancient colour. We skip the account of the hero's great-grandfather, who was so manly and honourable a lawyer in a country town.

Now the greatest and boldest tribute that can be paid to Hugo, the greatest and boldest, perhaps, that can be paid to any novelist, may be stated in the form that it is not safe to skip these passages in a novel by Victor Hugo. In other novelists all these details are dead; in Hugo they are all alive. In Hugo we may be certain that the sandy waste will be made typical, in some wild way, of the type and tribe of characters to which it gives birth; we may be certain that the furniture in the room will be packed with symbolism like an antique chapel. There will be something human and horrible about the tree, something significant and psychological about the three-legged stool. This is no exaggeration; in this sense it is literally true that there is not a dull line in Hugo.

The description of the wooded Breton country in *Quatre-Vingt-Treize* is really a string of primeval epigrams about the effect of the forest-darkness upon the soul of man. The description of the room of the Duchess in *L'Homme Qui Rit* is really a riot of a kind of bestial mysticism and of evil sanctities, such as might have filled some forgotten Phallic temple. This is the first and most admirable thing about Hugo as a novelist—that he is always interesting, and interesting for the best and most impressive reason, that in everything, however small, he is interested. Those parts of a novel, scenery, minutiæ, explanations, which in most novelists are the most tedious, in him are almost the most fascinating. He takes the details which the best authors alive are forced to make too tame and too long, and at the end our complaint against him is that they are too brilliant and too overstrained. Where none else can be tolerably vivacious, he contrives to be intolerably eloquent. For to him there is neither a large thing nor a small one; he has abolished the meanest and most absurd of all human words, the word "insignificant": he knows that it is impossible for anything to signify nothing.

Thus in what is, as a work of art, perhaps his most successful novel, *Notre Dame de Paris*, the sumptuous and fantastic details of Gothic architecture are practically almost as alive as the people that pass underneath them. In the presence of the mazy background of pious sculpture that runs like a pattern through the tale, we have something of the same sensation which we have sometimes in looking at such a façade as that of Rouen Cathedral; the network of stone is so rich and changing that we can almost believe it to be continually in motion, rippling underneath like a sea, with writhing serpents and fluttering birds. Hugo's backgrounds are never "set-pieces". So again in *Quatre-Vingt-Treize* the background to the two or three central figures is the most appalling of all possible backgrounds—a sea of faces. Cimourdain and Lantenac and the young Republican soldier have to act as stern and simple a drama as any old Greeks in a glade or wood; but instead of acting it in the midst of a wood they act it in the midst of a mob. "A two-legged forest" Hugo would probably have said. But his subordinate features are always thus terrific if our eye falls upon them; he will slaughter millions to make an accessory. In *Les Misérables*, as in *Notre Dame*, Paris is almost the chief character of the novel. In *L'Homme Qui Rit* the best description is that of two very weird and fierce and inscrutable things—the sea, and the English aristocracy according to Victor Hugo. In *Les Travailleurs de la Mer* he spends a vast deal of trouble on the reality of the cuttle-fish, and very little on the possibility or probability of the gentleman who fights with him. Hugo is not a successful novelist according to the conception that a novelist must understand human nature. He does not even pretend to understand human nature; he is a poet, and boasts of understanding nothing; he glories in an astounded and uplifted ignorance. Human nature to Hugo was a spontaneous and unbegotten and thrilling thing, a thing like the lightning and the burst of song among the birds. He did not profess to have vivisected man in the modern manner. Man was to him an awful thing, a thing to fly from, as he must have been to the animals in Eden.

The manifest theatricality and vanity of Victor Hugo have undoubtedly interfered with his appreciation by English readers, for we English people have thoroughly embedded in our minds the idea that vanity is a morbid and fantastic thing, developed by a high degree of hyper-civilization. We think this although every one of us has constantly noticed vanity in a child of three. We think this although every one of us knows that savages are vainer than civilized men, and that even the bonnets of Bond Street are not more elaborately feathered than the head-dresses of the Cannibal Islands. The truth is that Hugo represents all the ultimate and fundamental things—love, fury, pity, worship, hatred, and consequently, among other things, vanity. Vanity is not only not the same thing as self-consciousness, it is very often the opposite of it. When a man becomes self-conscious he very often becomes painfully and abominably humble. But so long as a man is healthily unconscious he is almost certain to be healthily vain. He will take a delight, without a moment's *arrière pensée*, in any of his own powers or characteristics. Hugo had, more than any other great man of modern times, this self-enjoying faculty. To him delight in himself was the first condition of all optimism, and faith in himself the first condition of all faith. If a man does not enjoy himself whom he has seen, how shall he enjoy God whom he has not seen? To the great poet, as to the child, there is no hard-and-fast line drawn between the Ego and the Cosmos.

Anyone who has ever watched a child for the first five years of its life will know that when the human soul first awakens to the immensities of mere existence, the first thing it does is to begin to act a part. In that first movement of the child we see the great part of the literary and political history of Victor Hugo. He had in all things an innocent arrogance; he had, if a paradoxical but accurate phrase may be employed, an utterly unconscious self-consciousness. And this quality fitted him supremely to be the expression of France in the nineteenth century; for France, having renewed her youth in that century, was really young. She had not only the fire and anger and hope of youth, she had also that more obvious and more painful characteristic of youth, its cleverness. *Quatre-Vingt-Treize*, the great novel of the Revolution, was not the most successful, perhaps; it was possibly the most Hugo-esque of the works of Hugo; for Hugo was supremely at one with the spirit of the Revolution, and his novel, like the Revolution itself, was one mass of epigrams. The story of the Revolution, indeed, gives an exceedingly good example of how misleading are many of the narrow English notions about sincerity and affectation, and how artificial is their idea of artificiality. If an Englishman read in a novel by Victor Hugo that a man about to be beheaded asked permission to take leave of a friend, and when forbidden exclaimed in a resonant voice, "Our two heads will seek each other in the sack," he would say that it was a monstrous example of Hugo's exaggeration. In the best style of the latter-day realist and psychologist he would point out how impossible it would be for a man paralysed with the last proximity of death to have his wits polished for such neat and fantastic discourse. If he read it in a novel of Hugo's, in short, he would say that it showed all the weakness of Hugo; but as a matter of fact it does not occur in a novel of Hugo's, but in the actual history of the French Revolution. The words were the precise words, attested by numerous witnesses, used on this prosaic earth of ours by a living man, Georges Jacques Danton, within ten minutes of becoming a dead one. Until we have realised this fact about the Revolution, all criticism of Hugo must remain vain and superficial.

Forms of expression always appear turgid to those who do not share the emotions they represent : thus the Hebrew songs appeared turgid to Voltaire and the critics of the eighteenth century ; thus the epigrams of the French Revolution appear turgid to ourselves. The reason is not that the Hebrew psalmists or the French Revolutionists were affected, but that we are not so interested in religion as the Hebrew psalmists, nor so interested in democracy as the French Revolutionists. The great demagogues of the Terror were so filled with the unifying convictions, that their life became a poetical unity, a work of art like the legend of a medieval saint. The extravagant appropriateness of Hugo's conversations are thoroughly in harmony with the extravagant appropriateness of the actual incidents of that period of French history. If Hugo does not honestly copy the Revolution, the only possible alternative is the somewhat improbable one that the Revolution honestly copied Hugo.

The second of the misunderstandings which interfere with the general appreciation of Victor Hugo is the misunderstanding of his idea of Republicanism or democracy. He appears at the first glance, from our point of view, a furious poet and an ineffectual politician, who was exiled from his country by the decision of a Bonapartist majority of his countrymen. He never ceased from calling down curses on the majority which was the basis of his own political creed, he never ceased from clamouring and praying for the rule of the very people whose decision had set him upon a lonely rock in the Channel. To the ordinary eye of these days nothing can be more pitiable than the position of the unpopular democrat. There is nothing more contemptible, at the first glance, than the man who has appealed, as Hugo appealed, from the people to a tyrant, and who finds immediately that the people and the tyrant are indissolubly allied against him. But to misunderstand Hugo on this point is to misunderstand the whole idea of democracy as Hugo understood it.

If there be one thing more than another which is true of genuine democracy, it is that genuine democracy is opposed to the rule of the mob. For genuine democracy is based fundamentally on the existence of the citizen, and the best definition of a mob is a body of a thousand men in which there is no citizen.

Hugo stood for the fact that democracy isolated the citizen fully as much as the ancient religions isolated the soul. He resisted the rule of the Third Napoleon because he saw that it had the supreme and final mark of the rule of the tyrant, the fact that it relied on the masses. As if a million of the images of God could by any possibility become a mass. He made his appeal to the individual, as every poet must do, and asked the solitary citizen to act as if he were really not only the only human being on the earth, but the only sentient being in the universe. He realised the obvious and simple truth, so often neglected, that if the individual is nothing, then the race is nothing—for the plain mathematical reason that a hundred times nought is nought. Therefore his sublimest figure, his type of humanity, was not either a king or a republican, but a man on a desert island.

THE GREAT GUSTO

IN CONSIDERING Dickens as a Victorian, perhaps the first necessity is considering him as a Pre-Victorian. It is not so much a matter of dates as of derivations; it must be remembered, to begin with, that he is much less completely inside the period, much less covered at both ends by the conventions of the period, than many great men whom some would call more original, like Ruskin or Meredith or Browning. On this side, indeed, Dickens is outside the Victorian enclosure, not so much because he was original as because he was traditional. Though labelled Radical, where others were labelled Tory, he carries on a rank, rowdy, jolly tradition of men falling off coaches, before the sons of Science and the Great Exhibition began to travel primly on rails or grooves. He carries on the old English legend of the coarse and comic novels of Smollett and Fielding, and none the less because under the gradual pressure of Victorianism his work is still comic but no longer coarse. The sort of comicality that commonly went with coarseness is apparent enough, especially at the beginning, while many of the other Victorians seem to have grown up, not merely Victorian—but something that should be called Albertian. This is the first and perhaps the frankest phase of Dickens; and but for refinements that really started later than this phase, it might easily have been even more frank. It may or may not be right to call him a caricaturist. But certainly, considered as a caricaturist, he starts straight away out of the world of Gilray and Rowlandson; a world widely different from that of Du Maurier or even Keene. We hardly feel any such direct heritage of the old comic writers even at the beginning of the other Victorian novelists; because they are more completely Victorian. And before we come to the application of this fact to his fiction, it has some application to his life. For circumstances started him almost unconsciously with a certain very ancient tradition, which for special reasons had become a very English tradition. It makes an immortal appearance in his first great masterpiece of *Pickwick*, but it is connected also with something in his personal position as well as in his literary lineage. It is perhaps the simplest figure in which we can summarise his primary position both in life and letters. I will call it for convenience the great tradition of the Comic Servant. And though in special ways it had been softened by being Christian and emphasised by being English, it is a very venerable tradition, which works back to the position in antiquity of The Comic Slave.

To explain this, we may briefly allude to his life, though there is no space for his biography. He was born in Portsea, a part of Portsmouth, in 1812, but was soon removed to Chatham, around which neighbourhood his early life largely revolved. His father was an impecunious old party, whose occupation was often shadowy and what the hasty will describe as shady. But he was the model of Micawber, and therefore must have had in him something great and good. He and his son later went to London, where they both became Parliamentary reporters; but the son soon turned from reporting politics to reporting life. As a journalist he wrote under the name of "Boz", and certain sketches of his attracted attention; a friend and patron named Hogarth had a family of daughters, among whom he found first a wife and afterwards a friend; but his first great opportunity came with the offer to write a story round Seymour's sketches of the pranks of the Nimrod Club, which he managed to turn into the more famous

Pickwick Club. The book was hugely popular, and ever afterwards he was busy, successful, laborious, inventive, excited and exhausted until he died. *Oliver Twist*, which stands somewhat alone, was followed by a serial scheme of stories within a story called *Master Humphrey's Clock*, in which *Barnaby Rudge* and *The Old Curiosity Shop* both appeared. Later, at regular intervals, came *Nicholas Nickleby*, *Martin Chuzzlewit* and *Dombey and Son*; and with the latter we reach and recognise a change in his mood and method; the frank farce begins to fade away, and the more subtle, sober and realistic Dickens of later years develops. He reaches his most sincere moment in the semi-autobiographical *David Copperfield*; his most earnest social philosophy in *Hard Times*, with something of the same graver reforming spirit in *Bleak House*; and his most restrained and delicate artistic success in *Great Expectations*. *Little Dorrit* was something of an interlude; and then he gathered up into his last complete book, *Our Mutual Friend*, all his growing knowledge of the realities of society, of the growth of plutocracy and the peril now threatening the national tradition. His furious industry, combined with yet more devastating tours in America, to say nothing of the private tragedy that separated him from his wife, gave something gloomy and feverish to his end; and he died in 1870, leaving unsolved other mysteries besides *The Mystery of Edwin Drood*.

It is rather symbolic that he died in that year of Prussian victory, which was the eclipse of Liberty throughout the world. For he had grown up with the growing liberalism of England, and is perhaps the one great Englishman who consciously devoted himself to democracy, as a feeling as well as a theory. He stands for all the hearty humanitarianism of that age at its best; and yet there is a deeper and older element in him, which I have put first because it came first.

I mean what I have already called the tradition of The Comic Servant.

If we call Dickens democratic, we must qualify it by saying that he is the derisive democrat rather than the dignified democrat. If he looks down on worldly rank, it is not from the severe status of the citizen of antiquity ; it is not even from the solid status of the peasant in any peasantry. It is rather with that inverted and comic contempt, which looks down when it looks up. It derives, not so much from any levelling dogma that Jack is as good as his master, in the sense that he should have no master ; it derives rather from the old joke, found in many an old legend, that Jack is better than his master ; that in the last scene the last are first and the first last. We could hardly summon the solemnity to say that Samuel Pickwick and Samuel Weller are two equal citizens ; if only because in some ways the servant is the superior. But the superiority is the superiority of a comic servant, not of a master or even a peasant proprietor ; superiority in wit and satire and cunning, but not superiority in status or seriousness or dignity. Now despite the growth of more grave and ideal democratic views, this did long remain the real attitude of the real Dickens. He was, first of all, the poorer man making fun of the richer ; but instinctively using fun as his weapon, and not minding if in the process he seems merely the funny man. This was complicated afterwards, as will be noted later, by many less natural ambitions touching rhetoric and sentiment. But when Dickens is most like himself he is most like Sam Weller ; and least like Wat Tyler or William Tell. He is more really concerned to show that the tyrant is undignified than that the slave is dignified.

The point is that the comic Dickens existed before the tragic or melodramatic ; the comic was older than the tragic ; the comic was deeper than the tragic. It was partly because there was already a tradition of popular joviality rather than popular justice, of riot rather than revolt. It was partly because Dickens as an individual had lived for a long time amid this laughter of the populace, before he began to think more seriously of that social ideal; which is not merely the populace, but rather the people. Just as Sam Weller had run wild as a sort of guttersnipe, before he became a gentleman's servant and something of a philosopher, so Dickens had been one of the old English crowd, from which a nameless voice cries, "Three cheers for the Mayor; and may he never desert the nail and sarspan business as 'e made 'is money by", long before he had ever dreamed of seeing the tragic vision of a French crowd, as in *The Tale of Two Cities*, through the visionary eyes of Carlyle. That is the real comparison between Dickens the humorist and Dickens the sentimentalist, the sociologist, the realist, the reformer and all the many aspects that have been unfavourably or favourably compared with it. Not that his social criticism was bad, not even that his sentimentalism was always necessarily bad; but that his humour was the elder brother, more hardy, more mature, more expert and experienced; more genuine and more national and historic. For the English populace has lived on laughter; its substitute for religion, for property, and sometimes even for food.

We may say that in this matter there is a curious contrast with Scott. We may also say that in this matter Scott was really Scottish, and therefore the reverse of English. For the Scots, having a real religion of the people, have had a real dignity in the democracy. Nothing is more notable than this curious contradiction: that while Dickens called himself a Radical and really was a Democrat, and Scott called himself a Tory and really rejoiced in some qualities of the older aristocrat, Scott has a far nobler sense than Dickens of the natural human dignity of the poor. Small farmers or fishermen in Scott do not have to become comic servants in order to score off their masters; do not have to become Court fools in order to criticise the Court. They can be eloquent in plain words; they can be eloquent in poor man's speech; they can be eloquent in broad Scots. Nobody doubts the sincerity of Dickens or the justification of Peggotty; but they could not speak over the ruined hearth with the tongue of Meg Merrilees over the gipsy fires; a speech that almost rises into song. Nationality is not a matter of praise or blame, for by its very nature a nation gives a colour to things both good and evil; but it is important to realise that Dickens could no more have imagined Meg Merrilees than Scott could have invented Mrs. Wilfer.

Oddly enough, Dickens could only write good rhetoric when he meant it for bad rhetoric. When he himself seriously meant it for good rhetoric, it was generally bad. So completely was the comic spirit his spirit, almost in the sense of his soul, that anything he wrote with expansion and exaggeration was for him a liberation of the soul, and took on swelling contours of the comic, which really have their own beauty and even their own harmony. But when he was only making his serious characters dramatic, he often only made them melodramatic. When he was only stuffing the gaps of the mere story with serious matter, he was not enjoying himself so much; and the stuffing was often poor stuff. His fools could talk poetry, while his knaves could only talk sentiment. Therefore, strange as it may seem, the one or two occasions, on which Dickens may actually be said to be an English stylist, are those in which he is a satirist of what he considers a pompous and preposterous style. About as good a piece of English as he ever wrote in his life is Mr. Serjeant Buzfuz's speech, which is really an uncommonly good speech. We can see the difference at once, when we compare it with the really pompous and preposterous speeches he was putting, almost at the same time, into the mouths of his serious villains. For instance, *Nicholas Nickleby* is an early work ; but *Pickwick* is even earlier. But the raving of Ralph Nickleby is not even good as raving ; while the ranting of Serjeant Buzfuz is very good as ranting ; nay, is classical and almost rational as ranting. Few, I imagine, who have had business interviews with a money-lender, or even a stingy uncle, have ever heard him conclude the conversation with the words, "My curse, my bitter curse upon you, boy !" ; or formed a high opinion of his literary style if he did. But then Dickens was not enjoying himself in writing about Ralph ; and he was enjoying himself in writing about Buzfuz. Therefore, as I say, he so heartily enters into the real spirit of the old forensic eloquence and so fills it with his own ecstasy of emphasis, that he really writes a piece of good style worthy of a great stylist. After describing darkly how "a being, erect upon two legs and bearing all the outward semblance of a man and not of a monster", entered Mrs. Bardell's lodging-house, he has the art and restraint to close the passage with simplicity and severity : "This man was Pickwick ; Pickwick the defendant". Then, by a true stylistic inspiration, he starts afresh, as with a new paragraph ; "Of this man Pickwick I will say little. The subject presents but few attractions ; and I, gentleman, am not the man, nor are you, gentlemen, the men, to delight in the contemplation of revolting heartlessness and systematic villainy." Which is, quite seriously, a rattling good piece of English rhetoric ; a thousand times better than anything Dickens could have written when he wanted to be serious.

It would be an exaggeration to say that this is because Dickens was not serious about being serious. But it is true to say that his whole soul was seldom in anything about which he was wholly serious. He was a man with much of the actor in him; he was in fact an admirable amateur actor; the real sound old-fashioned sort of actor, who was proud of versatility and the taking of varied parts. When he took the part of a rhetorician or a sentimentalist or a social idealist, he was sincere as an actor is sincere; that is, as any other artist is sincere. He had something to say and he said it; not always perfectly, but often very well. But when he was describing something funny, he was himself. He was not acting but enjoying; he was almost the audience rather than the artist. There was something gigantic, as of the joy of a whole crowd, in his enjoyment. He was essentially the man who laughs at his own jokes, and his own jokes inspired him like wine to wilder and wilder creation; but always to the creation of beauty in his own department of the far-fetched and the fantastic. What is more to the purpose here, they could inspire him even in the department of the forensic or the classic.

In Dickens it is the man who is entirely in the wrong who invariably says the right thing. All the genius is in that saying of the right thing; that is, of the exquisitely and ecstatically wrong thing. His fun is a form of poetry; and quite as personal and indefinable as poetry. Like poetry, it is for the moment on one note, and making the most of one notion; like poetry, it leaves us amazed at what can be made out of one notion. That is what the critics mean who say it is not like life; because it is more living than life. It is a magic accelerating growth; so that one seed out of a thousand seeds of fact visibly springs and sprouts into a tree, as in a fairy-tale. Certainly this is not dealing with all the facts; but it is releasing all the potential life in one of them. Dickens saw something, whether in a man's notions or in his nose, which could be developed more than dull life dares to develop it. The Dickens comic character is in that sense real and in that sense unreal. We may call it a caricature; though indeed it is a caricature of Dickens to call him a caricaturist. The very criticism itself has the over-simplification of a caricature. But if anybody thinks that anybody can do it, that it is a vulgar trick of exaggerating anything, that it is not a work of art, that it is not a work of genius —then that critic may be curtly recommended to become a great comic novelist and create a score of Dickens characters out of the next twenty people he meets. He will soon find that he can no more do it than he can become a great poet merely by admiring the sunset. In this sense we may say that Dickens was really too subtle and distinguished; and that is why it was easy to call him obvious and vulgar.

We may here recur to the fact first stated; that Dickens, who was in a family sense almost as new and nameless as a foundling, or at least often almost as lonely as an orphan, had in a literary sense something like a pedigree. He called one of his sons Henry Fielding Dickens, and we instantly feel that he had a sort of natural right to make a godfather out of Henry Fielding; more than he had, in that sense, to make one out of a pure Victorian like Alfred Tennyson. But the comic literature was not all great literature, nor its exponents all men like Fielding; and there were two sides to the very broad farce prevailing before the time when the Tennysonian refinement finally prevailed. In some ways this crude comic tradition did him harm even then; and in one particular way it does him even greater harm now. It is notable that he took over certain stock stage figures, of the farcical sort, and many modern readers are still repelled by a general impression that the story is stale, before they go on to discover that the story-telling is almost startlingly fresh. For instance, they feel that it is not very funny that Mr. Tupman was a fat man who dressed up as a dandy and a lady-killer. It is not very funny; and for that reason Dickens really tells us very little more about Mr. Tupman. It marks the inspired inconsequence of his method, that the story of Pickwick is not chiefly the story of the Pickwickians. Dickens started with the stock characters, but he crowded the stage with superb supers who have nothing to do with the play, and who are the making of it. By the end, the story is full of entirely new and original characters, and none more new than Mr. Samuel Pickwick; who has somehow changed from a goggle-eyed old buffoon to a most mellow and well-mannered old English merchant.

Nobody does justice to Dickens the creative artist who has a general prejudiced impression of Dickens the caricaturist. He actually began with a commission to write what were little more than captions for caricatures. The point is that while the caricatures remained stiff or vulgar, the new captions grew more and more inventive and imaginative. The test is not in the situations, but in the treatment of the situations. There must have been many tipsy clerks, in many comic novels, who roystered in their cups in the manner of robbers carousing. But only one of them, whose name was Richard Swiveller, when crying "Some wine here, ho!" ever carried dramatic versatility so far as to hand the flagon to himself with profound humility and then receive it haughtily. There must have been many jokes about Valentine's Day as vulgar as the valentines, but only in the Weller family was there that remarkable debate on diction, which decided whether "circumscribed" or "circumwented" is a more "tenderer" word. Many allusions less than delicate were made to Mrs. Gamp's profession; but only one gave us a flashing glimpse of that distracted husband, and the invalid who was told "to ease 'er mind, 'is 'owls was organs"!

Nevertheless, Dickens did gain something essential to his greatness from that old tradition of England, and even from that relatively old tradition of revolution. I know not what it should be called; if I had to invent a name for it I should call it

The Great Gusto

The Great Gusto ; something whole-hearted and precipitate about the mirth and the anger of that age, when there were mobs and no ballot-boxes. When all is allowed for the many noble names that are native to the Victorian time as such, to their several forms of sincerity or self-direction, it is true that the great force, or even the great violence of Dickens flows through them all, like an ancestral river coming from older places and more historic hills. He is all the more traditional because he is ignorant. He has that vast silent incessant traditionalism that we call the ignorance of the populace. And it is right to say that when more sophisticated Victorians set up fads like fences, and established new forms of narrowness, that flood of popular feeling, that was a single man, burst through them and swept on. He was a Radical, but he would not be a Manchester Radical, to please Mr. Gradgrind. He was a humanitarian, but he would not be a platform Pacifist, to please Mr. Honeythunder. He was vaguely averse to ritual religion ; but he would not abolish Christmas, to please Mr. Scrooge. He was ignorant of religious history, and yet his religion was historic. For he was the People, that is heard so rarely in England ; and, if it had been heard more often, would not have suffered its feasts to be destroyed.

VANITY FAIR

THE rising generations, when confronted with *Vanity Fair*, as with the *Iliad*, the *Book of Job* or other works, are fully entitled to be struck, or even repelled, by the appearance of something old-fashioned; so long as they remember that they will not go on rising very long, before they become old-fashioned themselves. But in the matter of the form of fiction, fashions follow each other today with rather bewildering rapidity. *Vanity Fair* might have appeared somewhat formless to some of the old supporters of the classical unities; it might again have appeared somewhat formless to the exact artistry of the school and generation of Stevenson; but even if it were much more formless than it is, it could hardly reach the superb ecstasy of formlessness, which is admired in many of the long realistic novels of today. As a matter of fact, it is far less formless than it looks. The narrative style of the novelist is garrulous and therefore discursive. Indeed the way in which the tale is told is in a rather special sense the manner of gossip. It is gossip not only in being casual and allusive; but also in actually being indirect. Much of the story comes to us by rumour; tales are told by one club man to another club man; we might say by one Thackeray to another Thackeray. He often manages to suggest more than he is prepared to say, by putting up some jolly old snob to say it. The method of gossip has a certain realism; it suggests the same figure seen from many sides; like a single man seen in all the mirrors of the London club. It will at least be well if the younger critic realises that Thackeray's style, which seems to be one of drawling and dawdling irrelevancy, is not an accident but an artistic method, suitable to his special purposes; and that sometimes his very irrelevance is as relevant as a conjurer's patter. In more direct and economical stylists, such as Stevenson, we know what the author thinks of the character; and possibly what the character thinks of the other character whom he marries or murders with a cutlass. In books like *Vanity Fair*, it is very necessary that we should also know what the World thinks of the character; for indeed in *Vanity Fair* the chief character is the World. It would be an exaggeration to say that the World is the villain of the piece; but it may well be said that in this sense it is a novel without a hero. The theme of it is what the old comic dramatist called *The Way of the World*; and a sort of satiric but not too severe judgment on it, for the way in which it treats all its characters, including the comparatively rare heroes and villains. For this purpose it is necessary that the club of Thackeray, like the island of Prospero, should be "full of voices"; and that we should get a general sense of much that is mere talk, or even mere echoes. For instance; I doubt if it would have been possible to convey the historic but rather unique position of the few very great, because very rich, English Dukes or Marquises (who were something quite different from mere nobility or gentry, in the sense in which any squire or soldier might happen to have a title); it would have been impossible to suggest the strange public position of a man like Lord Steyne, without all those scattered allusions to him and momentary glimpses of him, in the distance, on the high places of English social life. That sort of man is Somebody through all the nobodies who never knew him. We should not feel it enough by being suddenly introduced into his presence; we have to feel that his very absence is as impressive as his presence. All this gossip about the great House of

Gaunt is deliberate and even delicate, and without it we should not get the distance or the perspective that points to the ultimate scene ; or feel the full force of that splendid blow which the obscure and stupid husband struck, leaving the scar which Lord Steyne carried till his death.

Allowing for this wandering style (which as I say is often artful as well as artless), I repeat that there is a real form in *Vanity Fair*, the lines of which are kept more carefully than in much modern fiction. The pattern or outline of the story consists of the parallel or divergent careers of two girls, who start together from the same school in the first chapter. Vanity Fair, or the fashion of this world that passes away, is tested by its treatment of these two types and tests the types in its turn. One is the celebrated Becky Sharpe, the adventuress with many of the attractions of adventure ; courageous, humorous, quick-witted, but under these natural defences somewhat hard and entirely cynical ; one of those children of the poor who are born with a curious moral conviction of a right to possess riches and to rob the rich. The other is a more normal young woman of the sort that most would call ordinary ; not demanding much from life, but expecting at the best a happiness of the sort called sentimental ; and in all her views of existence at the best traditional, and at the worst conventional. I may remark here that I think it was one of Thackeray's real mistakes that he made her hold on such things rather conventional than traditional. Indeed in this case he was too conventional himself. He was so occupied with his contrasted pattern, with the good golden-haired heroine on one side and the wicked red-haired heroine on the other, that he made the golden-haired heroine a great deal less heroic than she might reasonably have been. It is not stating the alternative of vice and virtue fairly to make the vicious person a wit and imply that the virtuous person must be a fool. If he had been less anxious to make her a pathetic figure, she would have been more of a tragic figure.

Indeed, I think one disadvantage about *Vanity Fair*, especially today, is that one or two of these weak exaggerations occur very early in the book : and some greater passages only towards the end. Amelia is made at the very beginning a mere pink and white doll to be a foil to Becky ; and if she represents a rather stale and vapid sort of sentimental comedy, her brother, Jos Sedley, represents a rather stale and vulgar sort of sentimental farce. I never could understand, even in youth, why that fat and featureless buck was allowed to sprawl across so much of the opening of the story ; and I think it is rather a false note to make Becky deliberately set her cap at him. I imagine Miss Sharpe as already knowing the world well enough not to waste herself on so socially fourth-rate a figure. It almost seems as if the Sedley family were more unfairly treated by Thackeray than by fortune ; since the brother is vulgarised merely that he may be a slightly more vulgar copy of the dandy Osborne ; while the sister suffers throughout from that first water-colour sketch of the two schoolgirls, in which Amelia is given all the water and Rebecca all the colour.

But, allowing for this, which I confess to thinking a mistake, we can still trace the clear outline and the largely convincing logic in the contrast of the two heroines. The contrast is of importance, for it involves the chief debates about Thackeray : the sense in which he was wrongly called cynical ; the sense in which he may rightly be called sceptical. First of all, any number of idiots doubtless did call him cynical, because the story of these two girls was not what they called a moral tale ; by which they meant the grossly immoral tale which tells, in the teeth of Job and Jesus Christ, the lie that the virtuous are rewarded with wealth. It is not, certainly, in that sense, a story of the Idle and Industrious Apprentice. It is certainly not modelled on the disgusting morals of "Pamela or Virtue Rewarded". But (and this is the important point) neither is it made to enforce the opposite modern moral of "Amelia or Virtue Punished". There are many twisted and poisoned writers today, who would have played out the whole play with the opposite anti-moral purpose; leaving the wicked Becky in the blaze of the candelabra of Gaunt House and the kind Amelia picking up bits of coal, with a smut on her nose. This tragic trick (which was only too attractive to Thomas Hardy) is quite as much of a refusal to see life steadily and see it whole as the opposite artifice of the most artificial happy ending. It is not probable, but improbable, that Becky, with her desperate double or triple life, would have remained the Queen of Society for ever. It is not probable, but improbable, that anyone with the virtues and old connections of Amelia would have found absolutely none of her old friends ready to patch up her life for her. The point is that it is a sort of patching up in both cases. And with that we come near to the real meaning of Thackeray and the real moral of *Vanity Fair*.

The general inference from *Vanity Fair* is that life largely deceives and disappoints *all* people, bad and good; but that there is a difference, and that is (though the stupid optimist could not see it) rather on the side of the good. If we judge even Becky's life by the ambitious flights and flirtations of the beginning she is a ragged and disreputable failure at the end. If we judge Amelia's life by the romantic hopes of her first engagement, she is a stunned and helpless victim at the end. But if we compare the failure of Becky with the failure of Amelia, we see something that is profoundly true and is the chief truth of *Vanity Fair*, though most of the critics have missed it. The simpler, more innocent and more bewildered person is still capable of settling down into some sort of consolation and contentment; whereas she who has hardened herself against scandal or remorse has also hardened herself against hope.

A good novelist always has a philosophy; but a good novel is never a book of philosophy. The moral philosophy of Thackeray unites him rather with the old moralists than with the modern pessimists. He says, as his favourite authors, Solomon and Horace, would say, that life is in a sense vanity. He would never admit, in the sense of more modern authors like Zola and Dreiser, that life is also vileness. His view may be called stoic or sceptic or anything else rather than pessimist. But because he was a novelist and a narrative artist, and not merely a man with a theory, it is true that there did appear in his works something of a personal note, not to be explained by any impersonal system. There is, when all is said and done, something which haunts the air and discolours the very scenery of *Vanity Fair* though it has never been satisfactorily stated or explained. It is a vivacious book, passing chiefly through scenes of gaiety and fashion; it is often witty and satirical; it contains a great deal of humorous interlude and comic characterization; some of it, as I have noted, being even too broadly comic. But it is not a *jolly* book; even when it is for the moment a funny book. There really is something about it faintly acid and antagonistic; and that something did belong partly to Thackeray the man, as well as to Thackeray the philosopher.

There is an awful human weakness, dating from the days of the Victorian novel but not at all unknown today, which drives men madly and blindly to make a comparison between Thackeray and Dickens. Humanity is apparently expected to divide into two parties, as if they were following two political leaders; and every man expected to adorn his coat with the red rosette of a roseate optimism more or less untruly attributed to Dickens, or else with the yellow rosette of a bilious cynicism equally incorrectly identified with Thackeray. It was never apparently hinted that man, being divinely endowed with free will and the use of reason, to the point of unreasonableness, was perfectly at liberty to like both Dickens and Thackeray, or to dislike both Thackeray and Dickens, or to enquire why he should be compelled to couple these two names at all, any more than those of Scott and Balzac or Tolstoy and George Eliot. In nine cases out of ten in which this comparison has been used, it is quite useless. In one particular point, in which it has not been used, it is really of some use.

If we want to understand the *tone* of Thackeray, the thing which is rather subtle and often misunderstood and makes up so much of the atmosphere of *Vanity Fair*, we must look first at something in his life and character, which can really be seen most sharply in contrast with that of Dickens. Dickens was a man who began in poverty and fought his way up to relative riches. Thackeray was a man who began with the reasonable prospect of riches, lost that prospect and had to work under conditions of relative poverty. With all his social type, tastes, and intentions, those of a gentleman of private means, or at least of considerable leisure, he became a hack and hung about Grub Street for a long time, before he had anything resembling the rapid rise and popularity of Dickens. It happened, as most people know, through his being ruined by professional gamblers, with whom he had played cards in his capacity of casual and lordly man of the world. The theme of such a swindle occurs again and again throughout his work, notably his minor works ; especially in the story of the dashing methods of the Honourable Percy Deuceace.

Now this did really involve a tone, which the comparison with the other novelist may make more clear. Money was a sore subject with Thackeray. But it was not so much a sore as an itch ; in the sense that he could not let it alone and was always irritating it anew. Money was not a sore subject with Dickens. What is much more important, *poverty* was not a sore subject with Dickens. It did not really depress him; because he had faced it from the first and triumphed over it long before the end ; and for both reasons he was familiar with it and not ashamed of it. Dickens does not describe the poor as merely unhappy, because he remembers being happy when he was young, and even when he was poor. The festivities of the families of Nubbles or Cratchit are perhaps the most successful pictures of positive happiness in human literature ; for it is a very difficult thing to describe. Now it is sometimes said that Thackeray confined all his attention to the rich and to being a mere novelist of society. This is meant for a sneer ; but I rather wish for his sake that it were a truth. The truth is that Thackeray often did describe dismal lodgings and dreary privations and even high life below stairs. But what he could not bring himself to believe was that the lodgings were not always dismal ; from the point of view of the lodgers. That is where the real difference from Dickens came in ; for, much as Dickens suffered in youth, the lodgings had once, for him, really been *home*. He knew that it was really possible for poor people to feel at home in them on Christmas Day. To Thackeray they had never been home, but a miserable seedy asylum for a man who had lost the home of his fathers or his equals. Hence it is not so much that Thackeray never looks at mean houses, as that he never looks at them from within ; there is written across all that part of his work the title of one of his tales ; *A Shabby Genteel Story*. Dickens was happier and more all of a piece ; partly because he had been more shabby and partly because he had never been so genteel.

In the particular case of *Vanity Fair* this tone can be easily caught in the description of the broken fortunes of the Sedleys; Dickens would never have thought that the Sedleys *were* so completely defeated by the Osbornes, merely because they lost a lot of money. But the paradox is that Dickens thought less of poverty because he had known it, and thought less of money because he had earned it. To have that particular Thackerayan tone, compounded of pity and acrimony, it is necessary to have a certain bitterness; which is the bitterness of the man who has lost money rather than of the man who has failed to gain it. This tone has been called pessimistic or stoical or helpless or a hundred things; it has been called cynical by the old, and sentimental by the young; and it has elements of all these things. But the essential of it, which determines the idea of *Vanity Fair*, is a certain feeling, which no novelist had yet really introduced into the fiction of England; though Balzac had already introduced it into the fiction of France. It would be putting it too simply to call it The Importance of Money. For it is also a particular sense of something ghastly and unnatural about the Importance of Money. It is the cry of somebody who has found out, by falling over it, or breaking it, or losing it, that it is important; and yet cannot reconcile its importance with his own inner dignity and right reason. Hence the metaphor which makes the whole apparent world a sort of show with booths and puppet-theatres: Vanity Fair. In a sense he could not *believe* in this world; as smaller sceptics cannot believe in the other.

For we may say of Thackeray what he said of Swift; that there did remain at the back of his mind, in spite of all apparent scepticism, a noble but rather dark reality that is of the substance of religion. The Victorian Age had made it vague; the tradition of classical scholarship had made it seem almost heathen; but it was there, by the unanswerable test that applies to all the prophets and the saints. Thackeray thought the world *false*; which alone proves the presence of something contrasted with it which is true. Despite the superficial irritability which I have described, and which accounts for some of his lighter and less convincing sneers, it is true that he was too great a man to be godless and that he did not in his heart doubt that the injustices of the earth stand in contrast with a real justice. That is why I say that he stands rather with the ancient moralists than with the modern pessimists. It is true that this phrase also has been used incessantly and invariably wrongly. He himself confessed to a tendency to moralise; and many modern readers will doubtless repeat with far fiercer contempt this charge of moralising. But as a fact, it is not moralising at all. It is not strictly even philosophising. It is repeating old proverbs like the burden of an old song. It is not surprising that people once called it cynical and now call it sentimental. "Oh, it's the old story" is a sentence that can easily be said, both in a cynical and a sentimental tone. Thackeray was penetrated through and through with the conviction that this story is only the old story; and no criticisms can anticipate him on that. But its importance is that, like many old stories, it is in its way a great tragedy; and tragedy is that point when things are left to God and men can do no more.

THE MORAL PHILOSOPHY OF MEREDITH

I HAVE just read a letter on the subject of Meredith and Dickens, which is very typical of all that we must throw off in the modern world or perish. Why anybody should want to compare Meredith and Dickens any more than Hesiod and Thackeray, I do not know. But the letter was to this effect; that Dickens could not really be a great artist, because in his books one could divide men into good and bad; and with Meredith, it was alleged (very unjustly) one could not do this. There could be no stronger case of that strange fanaticism which fills our time; the fanatical hatred of morality, especially of Christian morality. This attempt to condemn all working moral judgments in fiction was made the instrument of a eulogy upon Meredith. Meredith, it was suggested, exhibited his characters not only as compounded of good and evil, but always, I presume, compounded of them (by some strange coincidence) in equal quantities. Meredith did not offer good people or bad people, but merely people; like animals to be considered scientifically and (I suppose) coldly, without reference to any high crisis of the conscience or wars between heaven and hell. That was the claim made for Meredith.

This being so, it is plain that Meredith, like Browning, must be rescued from his admirers. And there could hardly be a better end to begin at than this simple matter of the allegation about ethics. It is an atrocious libel upon Meredith to say that he was scientific or purely psychological or even purely æsthetic. It is a black slander to say that he did not preach, or that his characters are not properly placarded as good and bad. They are; just as much and just as little as in Dickens or any other writer whose books it is endurable to read. Books without morality in them are books that send one to sleep standing up. Meredith at least was not of that sort; he was complex but quite the reverse of colourless. His convictions may have been right or wrong; but they were very burning convictions. Are there no ethical sympathies in *Harry Richmond*; no political sympathies in *Vittoria*? But the most famous case is, of course, the most crushing of all. Meredith did what Dickens never did. He wrote a Morality; a pure and stern satiric allegory for the lashing of one special vice. The Egoist is not a man; he is a sin. And, as in all the old and wholesome Moralities of the ages of faith, the object of fixing the vice on one man is really to fix it upon all men. We have all posed with the Egoist, just as we have all fallen with Adam. There is no character in Dickens which is symbolic and moral in that extreme sense and degree. Micawber is not Improvidence, Sikes is not Brutality, in the utterly naked and abstract sense in which Sir Willoughby Patterne is Selfishness.

What is interesting about Meredith, was not that he did not recognise right and wrong; but what things he thought right and what wrong, and how far he differed from the current conceptions of his society. He left the world in comparatively little doubt about these things, except in so far as his mere mode of expression was dubious or indirect. Fantastic as he was, he was a fighter; and when you have understood a Meredith sentence you will generally find it is a stab. The argument of Meredith is that our little lives always stagnate into hypocrisy or morbidity unless the general wave of the world continually refreshes and re-creates us, and he maintains that the gods are a necessity of man. He prefers to say the gods rather than God; but that is a nineteenth-century prejudice.

Since Christianity broke the heart of the world and mended it, one cannot really be a Pagan; one can only be an anti-Christian. But, subject to this deeper difficulty, Meredith came much nearer to being a real Pagan than any of the other moderns for whom the term has been claimed. Swinburne was not a Pagan; he was a pseudo-Parisian pessimist. Thomas Hardy is not a Pagan; he is a Nonconformist gone sour. It is not Pagan to revile the gods nor is it Pagan to exalt a street-walker into a symbol of all possible pleasure. The Pagan felt that there was a sort of easy and equable force pressing upon us from Nature; that this force was breezy and beneficent, though not specially just or loving; in other words, that there was, as the strength in wine or trees or the ocean, the energy of kindly but careless gods. This Paganism is now impossible, either to the Christian or the sceptic. We believe so much less than that—and we desire so much more. But no man in our time ever came quite so near to this clean and well-poised Paganism as Meredith. He took the mystery of the universe lightly; and waited for the gods to show themselves in the forest. We talk of the curiosity of the Greeks; but there is also something almost eerie about their lack of curiosity. There is a wide gulf between the gay unanswered questions of Socrates and the parched and passionate questions of Job. Theirs was at least a light curiosity, a curiosity of the head; and it seems a sort of mockery to those Christians or unbelievers who now explore the universe with the tragic curiosity of the heart. Meredith almost catches this old pre-Christian levity; this spirit that can leave the gods alone even when it believes in them. He had neither the brighter nor the darker forms of spiritual inquiry or personal religion. He could neither rise to prayer nor sink to spirit-rapping.

Yet he was a religious Pagan because he had that great and central sacramental idea which is the one thing which marks religion from all imitations of religion or false definitions of it. It is the thing which is in all things that *are* religions, Brahminism, or Mormonism, or Catholicism, or Thuggee, or Devil-worship; but which is not in any of the things that merely pretend to be religions, such as Ethical Societies or Higher Thought Centres. This element can only be called the materialism of the true mystic. Those who do not like it call it fetish-worship. It is the idea that to enter upon abstractions and infinities is to get further and further from the mystery; to come near some particular stone or flame or boundary is to get nearer and nearer to the mystery. All unsophisticated human beings instinctively accept the sacramental principle that the particular thing is closest to the general, the tangible thing closest to the spiritual; the child with a doll, the priest with a relic, the girl with an engagement ring, the soldier with a medal, the modern agnostic with his little scarab for luck. One can recall the soul of boyhood better by smelling peppermint than by reading about adolescence; one could talk for hours about a person's identity and still jump on hearing his voice; and it is possible for Putney to be a much more pathetic word than Memory. I have heard modern people talk of the needlessness of all the old rituals and reliquaries and the need for a simple religion of the heart. But their demand is rather dangerous, especially to themselves. If we really had a simple religion of the heart we should all be loaded with relics, and rituals would be going on all day long. If our creed were only of the higher emotions, it would talk of nothing else but special shrines, sacred spots, indispensable gestures, and adorable rags and bones. In short, a religion of pure good feeling would be a positive orgy of superstition. This seems to me excessive; I prefer a little clean theology to keep the thing within bounds. But the thing itself is the essence of genuine religion; every genuine mystic, even the diabolist, adores something material. In short, both the mystic and the mere philosopher agree that the spiritual is more important than the material considered in itself. The philosopher thinks that the spiritual lies very far beyond the material, like a remote landmark behind a plain. The mystic thinks that the spiritual is very close behind the material, like a brigand hiding behind a bush. Science is always saying that the other world, if it exists, is too distant to be seen. Religion is always saying that it is too close to be seen. The kingdom of heaven is at hand.

Meredith in this deep sense is a mystic, though perhaps a Pagan mystic. He is a mystic in so far that he is a materialist. In all his work there is the smell and taste of things; it is grass and not the ghost of grass; fire and not the shadow of fire; beer and not the chemical analysis of beer. Nothing is so fine in Meredith as the satisfying solidity of everything. The wind in which Clara Middleton walked is a real wind; the reader can feel it in his hair. The wine which Dr. Middleton drank is a real wine; the reader can get drunk on it. It is true that Meredith, when one does not understand him, appears like a bewildering filigree or a blinding spider's web; but this is a question of the difficulty of finding his meaning, not of what it is like when found. Meredith's language is indefensibly intricate; but it is Meredith's language, not Meredith. It is as if someone were saying something quite hearty and sensible in Hebrew. In this sense Meredith is not only vivid but almost outrageous; and many Meredithian ladies have simpered somewhat sadly over the amount of space devoted to the taste, fullness, flavour and bouquet of Dr. Middleton's wine.

Meredith made us feel the bodily presence of people as well as their spiritual presence; and even delighted in the very bodily, as in schoolboys. And all this is, I think, ultimately connected with his conception of the universe, vague or pantheist as many may call it. But Meredith was not a pantheist; he was a Pagan. The difference consists in this tremendous fact; that a Pagan always has sacraments, while a pantheist has none. Meredith always sought for special and solid symbols to which to cling; as in that fine poem called "A Faith on Trial", in which all his agonies are answered, not by a synthesis or a cosmology, but suddenly by a white cherry-branch in bloom.

THE HEROINES OF SHAKESPEARE

IT IS an odd thing that the words hero and heroine have in their constant use in connection with literary fiction entirely lost their meaning. A hero now means merely a young man sufficiently decent and reliable to go through a few adventures without hanging himself or taking to drink. The modern realistic novelist introduces us to a weak-kneed young suburban gentleman who varies dull respectability with duller vice, and consumes three thick volumes before he has decided which woman he will marry. And by the strange, blasphemous perversion of words, he is called " The Hero ". He might just as well, in reason, be called " The Saint ", or " The Prophet ", or " The Messiah ". A hero means a man of heroic stature, a demigod, a man on whom rests something of the mystery which is beyond man. Now, the great and striking thing about heroines like Portia and Isabella and Rosalind is that they are heroines, that they do represent a certain dignity, a certain breadth, which is distinct from the mere homely vigour of the Shakespearian men. You could not slap Portia on the back as you could Bassanio. There may or may not be a divinity that doth hedge a king, but there is certainly a divinity that doth hedge a queen. To understand this heroic quality in the Shakespearian women it is necessary to grasp a little the whole Elizabethan, and especially the whole Shakespearian, view of this matter.

The great conception at the back of the oldest religions in the world is, of course, the conception that man is of divine origin, a sacred and splendid heir, the eldest son of the universe. But humanity could not in practice carry out this conception that everyone was divine. The practical imagination recoils from the idea of two gods swindling each other over a pound of cheese. The mind refuses to accept the idea of sixty bodies, each filled with a blazing divinity, elbowing each other to get into an omnibus. This mere external difficulty causes men in every age to fall back upon the conception that certain men preserved for other men the sanctity of man. Certain figures were more divine because they were more human. In primitive times of folklore, and in some feudal periods, this larger man was the conquering hero, the strong man who slew dragons and oppressors. To the old Hebrews this sacred being was the prophet : to the men of the Christian ages it was the saint. To the Elizabethans this sacred being was the pure woman.

The heroic conception of womanhood comes out most clearly in Shakespeare because of his astonishing psychological imagination, but it exists as an ideal in all Elizabethans. And the precise reason why the heroines of Shakespeare are so splendid is because they stand alone among all his characters as the embodiments of the primal ages of faith. They are the high and snowy peaks which catch the last rays of the belief in the actual divinity of man. We feel, as we read the plays, that the women are more large, more typical, belong more to an ideal and less to a realistic literature. They are the very reverse of abstractions ; considered merely as women they are finished down to the finest detail. Yet there is something more in them that is not in the men. Portia is a good woman and Bassanio is a good man. But Portia is more than a woman : Portia is Woman and Bassanio is not Man. He is merely a very pleasant and respectable individual.

There are Elizabethan plays so dark and frightful that they read like the rubbish from the wastepaper basket of a madhouse. No one but a prophet possessed of devils, one might fancy, could produce incidents so abrupt and so sombre, could call up scenes so graphic and so unmeaning. In one play a man is forced to watch the murder of those he loves and cannot speak because his tongue is nailed to the floor with a dagger. In another a man is torn with red-hot pincers; in another a man is dropped through a broken floor into a cauldron. With horrible cries out of the lowest hell it is proclaimed that man cannot be continent, that man cannot be true, that he is only the filthiest and the funniest of monkeys. And yet the one belief that all these dark and brutal men admit, is the belief in the pure woman. In this one virtue, in this one sex, something heroic and holy, something, in the highest sense of that word, fabulous, was felt to reside. Man was natural, but woman was supernatural.

Now it is quite clear that this was the Elizabethan view of woman. Portia is not only the most splendid and magnanimous woman in literature. She is not only the heroine of the play, she is the play. She is the absolute heroic ideal upon which the play is built. Shakespeare had conceived, with extraordinary force, humour and sympathy, a man to express the ideal of technical justice, formal morality, and the claim of a man to his rights: the man was Shylock. Over against him he set a figure representing the larger conception of generosity and persuasion, the justice that is fused of a score of genial passions, the compromise that is born of a hundred worthy enthusiasms. Portia had to represent the ideal of magnanimity in law, morality, religion, art and politics. And Shakespeare made this figure a good woman because, to the mind of his day, to make it a good woman was to ring it with a halo and arm it with a sword.

THE TASTE FOR MILTON

OF ALL poets Milton is the one whom it is the most difficult to praise with real delicacy and sincerity of definition. Of all poets Milton is the one whom it is most easy to praise with mere facile phraseology and conventional awe. There is one thing about Milton which must have been generally observed—that he is really a matured taste, a taste that grows. Shakespeare is really for all ages, for all the seven ages of man. I was fond of Shakespeare when I crept unwillingly to school, and I am fond of him now when I can be more vividly described as a lean and slippered pantaloon. And I do not mean that as a child I was fond of his romantic tales merely; I was fond of his poetry, especially when it was entirely unintelligible. The open and rolling rhythm seemed to be speaking plainly even when I could not comprehend it. The huge heraldic imagery of red and gold was obvious, though I could not take it in. Members of my family who collect coincidences have assured me that I was small enough to run along the street and fall on my nose in the very act of saying the lines:

> Do not for ever with thy veilèd lids
> Seek for thy noble father in the dust.

Lines like

> Revisit'st thus the glimpses of the moon,

or like

> Still climbing trees in the Hesperides

were not only good poetry, they were good children's pictures like the cow who jumped over the moon, or the number of red herrings that grow in a wood.

But Milton at his best is absolutely nothing to childhood. I do not mean that children cannot enjoy Milton; children can enjoy the Post Office directory. That is the kingdom of heaven; to enjoy things without understanding them. But I say that children cannot enjoy the Miltonism of Milton; the thing that no one but Milton can do. A boy does not appreciate that wonderful and controlled style, which, like a well-managed war-horse, even capers and caracoles rather by restraint than impetus. A boy does not feel the lift of those great lines, as of a great eagle leaving the nest,

> That with no middle flight presumes to soar
> Above the Aonian mount.

I think a great part of the trouble which the ordinary mind has in appreciating Milton (or, rather, Milton in pleasing the ordinary mind, for please remember that the popular mind is much more important than Milton) lies in the mistake of always describing him as a pure and classical writer. Really he was a highly complex and in some ways too modern writer. The perfectly classical can be understood by anybody. No charwoman would say that the tale of Ulysses coming back in rags to the woman who had been faithful to him was not a touching tale. No dog-fancier in the street would be indifferent to the death of Argus. No man in the street could ever say upon his conscience that the Venus of Milo was not a fine woman.

It is the secondary and distorted art which really and suddenly loses the sympathies of the people. The charwoman would fail in seeing the peculiar pathos of Mr. Robert Elsmere, who wanted to be a curate and also an agnostic.

The Taste For Milton

The dog-fancier would be justly indifferent to the rhetoric of the numerous modern animal lovers who could not look after a dog for a day. And the man in the street will not admit that the women of Aubrey Beardsley are fine women, because they are not. The tastes of the man in the street are classical.

And if Milton were really as straightforward as Homer or the Elgin Marbles he would be, in practice, uproariously popular. The real reason that he cannot make his glory quite as broad as it is undoubtedly deep and high is that there was in him something of the modern individualist, something of the social schismatic. He had that weird and wicked ambition of the modern artist; he wanted "to think for himself". But Dante and Dickens wanted to think for other people also.

Milton stands between the very social society in which Dante lived and the very social society which Dickens always desired and occasionally experienced, with that fastidious isolation which belongs to art in our time and belonged to religion in his time. He is the seventeenth-century individualist. He is the perfect Calvinist; the man alone with his God. He is also the perfect artist; the man alone with his art. No man, perhaps, has ever had such power over his art since the arts of humanity were made. And yet there is something that makes one turn to the firesides of the *Pickwick Papers*, and even to the fires of the Purgatorio.

WILLIAM BLAKE AND INSPIRATION

MUCH has been said about Inspiration, especially in works of imagination, by authorities whom I profoundly respect and with whom I violently disagree. For one thing, it is commonly regarded as a religious or spiritual view of art to suppose that it does not come from the artist. It is implied that only a cynical, or at least a mundane view of it, would suggest such a profanity as that it does come from the artist. And this, to begin with, seems to me to be based on a bad religion and philosophy. We are supposed to rejoice unreservedly in the idea that a spirit has inspired what would otherwise be only a man. But it is really a blasphemy to talk about a man being "only a man". And it is really a heresy to talk of it as if a spirit must always be better than a man. A good man might possibly be prompted by a bad spirit; and in any case a man is himself also a spirit. And it seems to me nearer to the true Christian tradition to hold that man creates in his capacity of the image of God; and he is in nothing so much the image of God as in creating images. On the other hand, it is by no means impossible that such direct and all but divine creation might be deflected and confused, if he merely listened to all the loose elemental forces that might be wandering about in the universe. It seems to me that this did, in fact, very often happen, in the actual history of literature. Very great men have certainly talked of being inspired, but I doubt if it was when they were most great.

To take a famous case, William Blake certainly did claim that his works were sometimes dictated by more exalted spirits.

But what works did the exalted spirits dictate? With the most polite apologies to them, and with the warmest and even wildest admiration for Blake, I think that any impartial person, reading steadily through some of his most specially inspired Prophetical Books, will form a rather low opinion of the lucidity and capacity for connected narrative shown by the presiding angels. It is typical of the whole trouble that he was often eager to explain that his favourite angels were really devils. But he did not mean that they were bad ; he meant something else in a symbolic or cabalistic system of his own, in which words did not mean what they are supposed to mean. He meant, for instance, that devils stood for the divine principle of energy and angels for the divine principle of wisdom. But nobody reading his mystifying but amusing notes can say he was on the side of the angels. He is disposed rather to sniff and even to sneer at angels, preferring the more energetic department ; and he refers affectionately to one of his familiar spirits in the phrase : " This angel, who is now a devil, is a great friend of mine." All this occult cryptogram is very interesting in its way to those who like the Gnostic type of theology. But when we talk of a poet being inspired, we imply that he is inspired to poetry. And nobody shall persuade me that this tangle of dogma and doggerel is an improvement on Blake's poetry—

> O sunflower weary of time
> That countest the steps of the sun.

Those two lines rise with the sweep and curve of a bird ; and I doubt whether any Gnostic devil was needed to dictate them. But the reader weary of time, who counteth the steps of reasoning in the densest parts of Blake's more metaphysical volumes, will feel a great deal less like a bird and a great deal more like a snail. I know well that there are in these books interesting and original ideas, because Blake was an interesting and original man. But such a man, if he is helped, should be helped to express himself. And I fancy that, when the devils left him to himself, he expressed himself much better.

I know that I have against me here, at least apparently, some of the things in which I am most proud to believe. I know that mythology is always true, or at least largely true: a great deal more true than the scientific study of myths. I believe profoundly in tradition; and there certainly is a great tradition of the poet and the Muse. Therefore, I speak tentatively; but even here I would tentatively suggest a correction. There is something that very few modern men understand, which I can only call the Levity of the Classics. The Classics are always treated as heavy, and therefore treated heavily; but there is a sense in which they should always be taken lightly. The men of the older civilizations had a certain subtle and mellow habit of mind, which has largely been lost in the dry earnestness of modern debates. They often dealt with things in which they only half-believed; and they somehow understood how to distinguish them from the things in which they really believed. That is why the men of the Renaissance, and even the men of the Middle Ages, could keep up a Pagan imagery running parallel to their Christian imagery. Chaucer will make his Knights worship Venus and Mars without the least sense of dislocation with the loftier passage, only a few pages after, in which the Duke of Athens celebrates the Christian Sacrament of Marriage in words that seem to come straight out of St. Thomas Aquinas. Shakespeare will have the same marriage celebrated by Hymen, the heathen goddess, and within a few lines of the same play talk of the sinner having retired to a monastery under the influence of a holy hermit. It is the same with the expression of many philosophical moods or spiritual emotions. These great traditional poets often express an idea of *Vanitas vanitatum* which might be mistaken for despair, and which in a modern writer probably would be despair. Yet in their religion despair was itself a mortal sin. They did not quite mean what they said; and they had some elusive lyrical faculty for suggesting that they did not quite mean what they said. The men of the old European culture could take pessimism lightly. The men of the new American culture can only take optimism heavily.

In this spirit all these poets claimed inspiration by a Muse, and there was something in what they said; but it was not exactly what they meant. It was not exactly meant as it would have been meant by somebody engaged in Psychical Research or claiming to be a Medium under a Control. The two successive ideas of serious Christian belief and serious scientific discovery have sharpened our minds to the definite question of whether a thing is strictly true. I am sure the old poets used the image of a Muse in a vaguer sense. Homer began by invoking the goddess; but I fancy he would have been very much annoyed to be told that he had not really composed the great speech of Sarpedon. And even Milton, though claiming inspiration from the Holy Spirit, would have been distinctly cross with the suggestion that anybody had written the invocation to Light except himself. In this vaguer sense, of an inspiration from God and Nature flowing into the personality, the conception is, of course, entirely true and valid. But in these days of psychic phenomena, or renewed mythology, it may be well to keep Inspiration within bounds.

A GRAMMAR OF SHELLEY

A SEVERELY scholastic text-book of the poems of Shelley, in a hard and ugly cover, with notes at the end of each poem explanatory of the difficult words, appeals to the literary instinct as a somewhat incongruous and fantastic thing. It is like a whole public school with all its masters and head-master going out in search of the key at the foot of the rainbow. Shelley was only the earthly name for a spirit that every vivacious child must meet once, if only once, and must meet alone. He is not a companion for the road of life, not a philosopher, not a prophet, not, properly speaking, even a man. But that we have each of us found him once for ourselves suddenly in some silent field has left in us a strain of salutary wildness without which we should have been Brixton burgesses to our dying day. That a spirit so valuable and so unreliable with whom we can no more agree or disagree than we can measure a cloud with a yard measure should be hacked up into squares and sections for Class I or Standard III is sufficiently curious. We do not envy the task of the compiler of the notes, who has to state in simple language what Shelley meant, which Shelley himself would have found it uncommonly difficult to do. But if these pedantic mutilations are indeed to be permitted and these prosaic paraphrases and synonyms piled up in the notes, the thing should at least be done well and carefully.

A great curse has fallen upon modern life with the discovery of the vastness of the word Education. Men have discovered that singing and wandering, the toys that are broken and the flowers that are plucked and thrown away, the dreams that have no archetype and the projects that have no fulfilment, are parts of one great thing that is called Education—education which in older and somewhat plainer language would have been called " the saving of a soul ". But in many modern educationists the effect of this great discovery has been precisely the opposite to that which it should have been. Instead of making Greek and geography as healthy as " Hunt-the-slipper " they have set to work to make " Hunt-the-slipper" as mechanical, as coercive, as meanly conscientious as Greek and geography. The new lesson should have made them see the ancient studies as the ancient scholars and humanists saw them, as ventures full of youthful freedom and magnanimity, parts of what was called in a fine and significant old phrase " a liberal education ". Instead of that, they have put the very follies of childhood into unimpeachable grammars and constructed, out of wind and sunshine and the truant impulse and the caress for the wild beast and bird, the most illiberal education that the world has ever seen. Let anyone who thinks such a description too strong to be appropriate turn to the last page of an edition of Shelley, which is called " Teaching Exercises ". The first question is as follows :

> Discuss the suitability of the following expressions : lips of lurid hue ; 'lorn bard ; bright silver dream ; deeper solitude ; the caves of divine sleep ; elemental diamond ; arrowy odour ; coming bulk of death ; . . . keen pyramid ; aerial merriment ; webs of melancholy mirth ; lulled by the coil of his crystalline streams.

I must admit that, just as Mr. Pecksniff would have liked to know Mrs. Todgers' notion of a wooden leg, I should very much like to know the ordinary schoolboy's notion of an " arrowy odour ". It would be interesting to possess the answer of any set of average pupils as to the suitability of " 'lorn bards " and " bright silver dreams ". But the vital objection to this question about the suitability of certain poetic phrases does not lie in the fact that no children could answer it, it lies in the fact that nobody in the world can answer it. Pleasure in the beautiful is a sacred thing; if a child feels that there is an indescribable witchery in the wedding of two words he feels it alone, as he feels his vanities and his dreams, in places where he cannot be badgered or overlooked or philosophically educated. The act of insisting upon his analysing the holy thing, I think, without the smallest doubt or the smallest desire to exaggerate, is as insolent as asking him to dissect his favourite kitten or account for his preference for his mother.

Such a project is especially absurd in the case of Shelley. It is possible to read Chaucer with a view to language or Milton with a view to theology, though the proceeding is not much more sensible than reading the *Odyssey* in order to learn navigation or " Jack and the Beanstalk " in order to study the habits of plants. But Shelley's works are not concerned, I do not say with material ideas, but scarcely even with material symbols or incidents. The whole of his work amounts to a great epic about an inspiring example of nothing in particular that was done nowhere in particular at no particular time. It was entirely consistent with this characteristic that he considered the Universe as the most exquisite masterpiece ever constructed by nobody. He was, as it were, a dealer in all disembodied good. He was an instinctive optimist, and thought that the Universe could contain every good thing except a deity. It is remarkable how Shelley and the school to which he belonged reconciled the optimism of their natural philosophy with the unflinching pessimism of their view of political institutions. At first sight one would think that the optimist would be a conservative. It is a strange truth that no force has been so disruptive and iconoclastic, has torn up so many ancient roots and pulled down so many holy places, as contentment with the world. Pessimism has never been a force, not even a destructive one. Before a man like Shelley could heartily disbelieve in a College Synod or a Lord Chancellor he had first heartily to believe in a whole Universe. In order to reconcile their two positions as the praisers and the denouncers of things, the school of Shelley fell back upon that extraordinary theory of the cunning of priests and kings—the theory that several centuries of human history had been occupied in the conduct and continuation of one prolonged hoax. The thing when realised is vastly more incredible than the legend of St. Denis. The Shelleyites never realised that it is the people who make the priests, and that all kings, including Nero, are elected by universal suffrage. They did not realise that, whether for good or evil, kings and priests were in their season as natural blossoms upon the tree of life as birds or babies, even if they were often as stupid as the babies and as cruel as the birds. This pasting down of whole pages in the book of man, this outrageous expurgation of history, seriously impaired the validity of Shelley's view; that it only impaired it is because that view was in itself essentially universal and full of faith. Few men in the world's history had more faith than Shelley. He had faith in the end of the most earthquake speculations, in the licence of the most confounding passions. Indeed, he could bring himself to have faith in anything except in the faiths of everybody else.

POETRY—OLD AND NEW

ONE of the new theories about poetry is that the poet must seek to isolate an image, and even a word. He must, to use the military phrase, cut all its connections and leave it in the air. To begin with, this interests me in the most superficial sense; because what strikes me about poets is that they were all hopelessly traditional, even when they tried to be revolutionary. Nobody could be more entirely in the air, to all appearance, than Shelley. Nothing could be more entirely in the air than his little pet, the Skylark. And no mind could be more filled with the conviction that it was completely in revolt against all tradition, and especially against all religion. And yet it would be quite an amusing exercise to take Shelley's poem about the Skylark, line by line and verse by verse, and show how entirely dependent it is upon traditional ideas, and even rather specially upon religious ideas. Here perhaps it would be rather too long an exercise to work my way through that rather long poem. But it is really true that it could be analysed, point by point, in that traditional sense. The song of the radiant young atheist would probably turn out in the end to be a most orthodox theological tract. He begins by saying, "Hail to thee, blithe spirit". What does he mean by talking about spirits, if he is not in any sense a spiritualist? What would be the meaning of the remark, if he were really a materialist? He would never have had even the idea of a spirit, but for the religious tradition represented in the idea of the Holy Spirit. He then says, "Bird thou never wert"; which is obviously a lie. But it is a lie symbolising a truth; and what he really means by it may be stated thus : " I refuse to believe that a bird is only a bird, or that there is nothing more in such things than the material facts that we know about them." That thought is the beginning of all theology. Shelley's next surrender to superstition is absolutely abject and appalling. He says, " from heaven, or near it " ; a remark which must make all modern and rational persons with one concerted movement cover their faces in shame. In plain words, he not only talks as if there were something divine in the mere empty space above our planet. He actually talks as if there were a paradise of saints and angels somewhere located, like a coloured cloud, in that space ; so that a skylark could be said to be more or less near to it. The lapse is so distressing that I will not linger upon the minor barbarism of medieval physiology, by which the emotions of the bird are represented as coming from its " heart "; as if that organ were a centre of consciousness. I was going to say that I " had not the heart " to dwell any longer on the depressing orthodoxy of Shelley ; whereby I should myself have fallen into the physical image that is so superstitious and medieval. It is so very difficult to write any intelligible English without being superstitious and medieval.

Needless to say, the criticism could not only be continued through the whole poem, but it becomes conspicuously clear and true in the most poetical parts of the poem. Certainly the finest passages, and perhaps the most frequently quoted passages, are those that really celebrate what is not only a Christian dogma, but one now often abandoned as an antiquated and benighted dogma. Those great movements of verse do not really correspond to the Rise of the Skylark, but rather to the Fall of Man. I daresay Shelley would have been very much surprised, if he had been told that he was subscribing to the doctrine of the Fall of Man. But he certainly was ; and that was why his words at that moment really become weighty and human. " We look before and after and pine for what is not ", has the sound of a great tolling bell. Nobody needs to be told that some spiritual tragedy has already happened to the race of him who cries aloud :

> But if we could scorn
> Hate and pride and fear ;
> If we were things born
> Not to shed a tear.

or to the poet who can compare such a tragedy with the more trivial bliss of a little feathered creature in the empty air.

At the very beginning of the debate, therefore, and even on the face of it, I have generally noticed that in the past all the poetry that professed to be particularly revolutionary was in fact particularly traditional. In this and in many things most of the revolutions of the past were pretty much alike ; and there are some of us who rather doubt whether the revolutions of the future will be particularly different. But even if we ignore this tradition of traditionalism, and suppose that the futurists have really something novel in the way of a novelty, the logical difficulty of their position still remains. We may, for the sake of argument, treat this change as if there had been no other changes. We may isolate the Imagist as he would isolate the image. We may treat the art as if it had no history ; just as the artist tells a story as if it had no beginning. But the fact still remains that, since he has to use the words of some language, he has got the words from somewhere and learned them from somebody. And the words are in fact winged or weighted with the thoughts and associations of a thousand years. If they were not, he would not use them ; he might just as well say " Grunk ", or " Quoggle ".

Poetry—Old and New

I have just read an example given by Mr. Humbert Wolfe of the sort of detached poem that the admirers of detachment chiefly admire. I may remark that Mr. Wolfe does not especially admire it; in fact he calls it a meaningless anecdote. But he is undoubtedly right in classing it as an example of the sort of thing that the school in question regards as the necessary isolation and intrinsic value of an image. Its substance is as follows; a Japanese general whose long trousers are twisted like corkscrews sees a European army pass, in the middle of which is a bishop who has one or two hairs on his chin and water in his eyes. That is all. The message is conveyed. The revelation is complete. Now I would not affect to misunderstand any notion that may require a little understanding. And I take it that even the poet would admit in such a case that, in a certain sense, the pointlessness is the point. The Japanese standpoint is selected because it is distant and indifferent; the bishop because, from such a standpoint, he is only a dull detail and nothing else. But even this effect still depends upon tradition and association. It would not be the same if the bishop were a biscuit-manufacturer. It would not be the same if the Jap were a Jewish army-contractor. It is because of what the bishop is to us that we remark that he is something different to the Mongol; it is even because he is something to us, that we note that he is nothing to somebody else. Even by this method of the detached detail, of the fragment of fact, of the experience isolated from all its surrounding experiences, we do not really get rid of the traditional might and magic in the words that are used to describe it. I suspect, therefore, that there is something wrong after all in the metaphysics of the new poetry; and that it is, much more than it fancies, in traditional continuity with the old poetry. The effect of callous and colourless record, produced by the picture of the Jap staring coldly at the bishop, is really every bit as much dependent on the long literary legend about the mystical priesthood and the mysterious East, as if it had been the most passionate battle-hymn of charging Crusaders, carrying the emblazoned Cross of a Prince Bishop against the banners of the Rising Sun.

BROWNING AND HIS IDEAL

ROBERT BROWNING has been called a religious teacher, to which objection can be raised, for, generally speaking, a poet cannot be properly appreciated if we separate one of his functions from the rest. Poets represent to a greater degree than any other men the conception of the unity of things. The poet includes the theologian, but he also includes the butcher, the baker, and the candlestick-maker. It is one of the curses of the criticism of poetry that it tends to detach the ideas of a poet from the forms by which he expresses them, which is like detaching the abstract idea of vegetation from all conceivable forms of vegetables. It is entirely useless to attempt to discuss the philosophy of Robert Browning apart from his poetry. The project is quite as ridiculous as the project of explaining the inspirations of Turner to a blind man, or of making the peculiar gospel of Wagner or Chopin clear to a deaf one. There is something in Turner beyond paint and turpentine, there is something in Wagner which could not be expressed by any instrument. But to describe the message of Turner without ever mentioning chrome yellow or flake white, to convey the importance of Wagner's work without any reference to the musical laws by which he worked, would be entirely ridiculous. It is nevertheless assumed that in literature the message can be detached from the words, a thing unknown in any other art.

This is more especially impossible in the case of Browning, because in him an intellectual revolution went hand in hand with an æsthetic one. It would be possible, indeed, to go further, and say that Browning's peculiar triumph consisted in the fact that he expressed normal truths with an abnormal accuracy, that he asserted in the language of a splendid revolutionist the feelings of an ordinary human being. It was by Browning's astonishing originality of technique that he really lent value to his virile and eternal ideas. Every religious writer had echoed the conception that all created things praise the Lord; but Browning was the first to take it literally as applying even to the grotesque and the unpresentable; he was the first to realise practically that hogs and monkeys praise the Lord. Those who speak, for example, of Robert Browning's neglect of form utter a wholly senseless criticism. Perhaps no English poet had as keen an instinct for form as Browning had. But form can be grotesque as well as dignified, ugly in the conventional sense as well as beautiful. A rhinoceros has as definite and unmistakable a form as a swan or a turtle dove; it would be no worse to set the rhinoceros' horn upon the swan than to clap the swan's wings on the rhinoceros. Even in the search after the fantastic there is a sense of form; even in artistic lawlessness there is a law. If any of those critics who think Browning indifferent to form imagine that they could write the "Soliloquy in a Spanish Cloister", or "Bishop Blougram's Apology", without possessing an artistic sense, there is nothing to be done or said except earnestly to recommend them to try. At a superficial glance the cathedrals of the Middle Ages appear often to be mere confusions of barbaric and almost demented sculpture in comparison with the frigid rectangular monuments of classical architecture. A very little knowledge, however, is sufficient to show us that it is amid these unbridled fantasies in stone that we find the swell and triumph of the great principles of engineering. Precisely in a similar manner we realise that all the flying buttresses and hideous gargoyles of Browning are portions of a great cathedral. The net effect of the work of a great artist is like the net effect of the works of Nature—it is conflict everywhere, and yet harmony above all.

The ordinary objection to Browning, the charge of needless obscurity, is just in a certain degree, yet requires a serious qualification. Browning is the simplest and most manly of poets in his message and intention. It is only his speech that is rough and quaint. There are writers of great depth and delicacy, such as Mr. Henry James, against whom the charge of obscurity is brought, but here the sense is very different. The writings of Mr. Henry James are obscure even when we understand them. They have to do (even as they are seen by the eyes of the author) with dim and fugitive and anomalous sentiments. But the moment that the cotton-wool of mere Philistinism is taken out of our ears the message of Robert Browning is a single trumpet calling thousands to the charge. He was only a splendid demagogue with an impediment in his speech. We speak, for the sake of convenience, of Browning being obscure; but it would be far truer to say that it is we who are obscure, hampered and blinded by elaborate and ceremonial speech, while he stands in the heart of the maze of life and speaks with an assurance which cows, and with an obviousness and simplicity which confound us.

There are certain central and important respects in which Browning is actually the simplest of all poets. No writer of his order of intellect that ever lived had the courage to be so direct and emotional—one might almost say, so babyish. If we turn to some of Browning's love-lyrics we find that he will take readily some figure of endearment, some phrase from the secret scriptures of folly, and write it boldly in blank isolation in the middle of a page:

> Aught like this tress, see, and this tress,
> And this last fairest tress of all,
> So fair, see, ere I let it fall.

It may be seriously doubted whether Shelley or Tennyson or Swinburne would ever have had the intellectual courage to compose, write down and leave untouched a lyric containing so much passion and so little of the faintest trace of thought or even common intelligence. Browning was a thinker, but he was not primarily a thinker. He had the courage to be everything—a prophet, a buffoon, a scholar, including the valuable courage to be a sentimentalist.

Odd as it may seem at first sight, the grotesqueness of Browning's poetry is definitely connected with this brazen emotionalism. In moments of strong feeling we do not speak in an exalted tone ; we curse and stammer like a man drenched with water or thumped over the head with a walking-stick. Browning was too passionate to be poetical. Passion makes every detail important ; there is no realism like the insatiable realism of love. Poetry is only the algebra of life ; passion is its arithmetic. If we recall to ourselves any deep sentiment ; if we think of a dead friend or a primitive attachment, it is a hundred to one that we shall not think of any poetic images, stars, or thrones, or angels, but of something utterly trivial and ugly—a railing, a door-knocker, a lost umbrella. Men talk foolishly of these things not rising into poetry ; on the contrary, it is poetry that falters feebly behind and does not rise to the graphic passion of these things. But scarcely any poet has come nearer to these queer memories, the veritable rag-bag of passion, than Browning in the incomparable realism of his love-poems. No one, surely, can forget the dark and gorgeous emotion of the lover groping his way to the seaside cottage in " Meeting at Night " :

> A tap at the pane, the quick, sharp scratch,
> And blue spurt of a lighted match.

It is that blue-flaring match that burns in Browning's poetry and endures after the wreck of all the eternal stars of Shelley.

It is the supreme misfortune of Browning that he has been chiefly expounded by men who bear as little resemblance to him as a circle of long-haired Parisian æsthetes could bear to Mr. Rudyard Kipling. He has been made a matter of painful intellectual study, when his own soul went always like a horse at full gallop or a river in spate. He has been presented as a riddle for the wise, when he himself first and foremost saluted the simple. The weedy and short-sighted "intellectuel" has found his chief pabulum in a series of poems which mean nothing if they do not mean that the essential merits are strength and spontaneity and the universal heart. Browning was, indeed, a logician, because he was a man and something much bigger and better than a poet. He was a logician because a logician is not, as is idly supposed, a frigid person, but a man hot for battle even in the æther of the abstract. A man must have loved much, must have loved God and men and animals, before he can really love even a distinction in terms. Browning loved reasoning as a man loves hunting or fencing or playing leap-frog, because it is an expansion and use of his powers. He had that lost and splendid attitude towards the things of the mind which marked the Middle Ages and the Renaissance. To him scholarship was one of the pleasures of youth; to know and reason was a delight and almost a dissipation.

TENNYSON

IT WAS merely the accident of his hour, the call of his age, which made Tennyson a philosophic poet. He was naturally not only a pure lover of beauty, but a pure lover of beauty in a much more peculiar and distinguished sense even than a man like Keats, or a man like Robert Bridges. He gave us scenes of Nature that cannot easily be surpassed, but he chose them like a landscape painter rather than like a religious poet. Above all, he exhibited his abstract love of the beautiful in one most personal and characteristic fact. He was never so successful or so triumphant as when he was describing not Nature, but art. He could describe a statue as Shelley could describe a cloud. He was at his very best in describing buildings, in their blending of aspiration and exactitude. He found to perfection the harmony between the rhythmic recurrences of poetry and the rhythmic recurrences of architecture. His description, for example, of the Palace of Art is a thing entirely victorious and unique. The whole edifice, as described, rises as lightly as a lyric, it is full of the surge of the hunger for beauty; and yet a man might almost build upon the description as upon the plans of an architect or the instructions of a speculative builder. Such a lover of beauty was Tennyson, a lover of beauty most especially where it is most to be found, in the works of man. He loved beauty in its completeness, as we find it in art, not in its more glorious incompleteness as we find it in Nature. There is, perhaps, more loveliness in Nature than in art, but there are not so many lovely things. The loveliness is broken to pieces and scattered ; the almond tree in blossom will have a mob of nameless insects at its root, and the most perfect dell in the great forest-house is likely enough to smell like a sewer. Tennyson loved beauty more in its collected form in art, poetry, and sculpture; like his own "Lady of Shalott", it was his office to look rather at the mirror than at the object. He was an artist, as it were, at two removes: he was a splendid imitator of the splendid imitations. It is true that his natural history was exquisitely exact, but natural history and natural religion are things that can be, under certain circumstances, more unnatural than anything in the world. In reading Tennyson's natural descriptions we never seem to be in physical contact with the earth. We learn nothing of the coarse good-temper and rank energy of life. We see the whole scene accurately, but we see it through glass. In Tennyson's works we see Nature indeed, and hear Nature, but we do not smell it.

But this poet of beauty and a certain magnificent idleness, lived at a time when all men had to wrestle and decide. It is not easy for any person who lives in our time, when the dust has settled and the spiritual perspective has been restored, to realise what the entrance of the idea of evolution meant for the men of those days. To us it is the discovery of another link in a chain which, however far we follow it, still stretches back into a divine mystery. To many of the men of that time it would appear from their writings that it was the heart-breaking and desolating discovery of the end and origin of the chain. To them had happened the most black and hopeless catastrophe conceivable to human nature; they had found a logical explanation of all things. To them it seemed that an Ape had suddenly risen to gigantic stature and destroyed the seven heavens. It is difficult, no doubt, for us in somewhat subtler days, to understand how anybody could suppose that the origin of species had anything to do with the origin of being. To us it appears that to tell a man who asks who made his mind that evolution made it, is like telling a man who asks who rolled a cab-wheel over his leg that revolution rolled it. To state the process is scarcely to state the agent. But the position of those who regarded the opening of the " Descent of Man " as the opening of one of the seals of the last days, is a great deal sounder than people have generally allowed. It has been constantly supposed that they were angry with Darwinism because it appeared to do something or other to the book of Genesis ; but this was a pretext or a fancy. They fundamentally rebelled against Darwinism, not because they had a fear that it would affect Scripture, but because they had a fear, not altogether unreasonable or ill-founded, that it would affect morality. Man had been engaged, through innumerable ages, in a struggle with sin. The evil within him was as strong as he could cope with—it was as powerful as a cannonade and as enchanting as a song. But in this struggle he had always had nature on his side. He might be polluted and agonised, but the flowers were innocent and the hills were strong. All the armoury of life, the spears of the pinewood and the batteries of the lightning went into battle beside him.

Tennyson lived in the hour when, to all mortal appearance, the whole of the physical world deserted to the devil. The universe, governed by violence and death, left man to fight alone, with a handful of myths and memories. Men had now to wander in polluted fields and lift up their eyes to abominable hills. They had to arm themselves against the cruelty of flowers and the crimes of the grass. The first honour, surely, is to those who did not faint in the face of that confounding cosmic betrayal ; to those who sought and found a new vantage ground for the army of Virtue. Of these was Tennyson, and it is surely the more to his honour, since he was the idle lover of beauty who has been portrayed. He felt that the time called him to be an interpreter. Perhaps he might even have been something more of a poet if he had not sought to be something more than a poet. He might have written a more perfect Arthurian epic if his heart had been as much buried in prehistoric sepulchres as the heart of Mr. W. B. Yeats. He might have made more of such poems as "The Golden Year" if his mind had been as clean of metaphysics and as full of a poetic rusticity as the mind of William Morris. He might have been a greater poet if he had been less a man of his dubious and rambling age. But there are some things that are greater than greatness; there are some things that no man with blood in his body would sell for the throne of Dante, and one of them is to fire the feeblest shot in a war that really awaits decision, or carry the meanest musket in an army that is really marching by. Tennyson may even have forfeited immortality: but he and the men of his age were more than immortal; they were alive.

Tennyson had not a special talent for being a philosophic poet, but he had a special vocation for being a philosophic poet. This may seem a contradiction, but it is only because all the Latin or Greek words we use tend endlessly to lose their meaning. A vocation is supposed to mean merely a taste or faculty, just as economy is held to mean merely the act of saving. Economy means the management of a house or community. If a man starves his best horse, or causes his best workman to strike for more pay, he is not merely unwise, he is uneconomical. So it is with a vocation. If this country were suddenly invaded by some huge alien and conquering population, we should all be called to become soldiers. We should not think in that time that we were sacrificing our unfinished work on Cattle-Feeding or our hobby of fretwork, our brilliant career at the bar, or our taste for painting in water-colours. We should all have a call to arms. We should, however, by no means agree that we all had a vocation for arms. Yet a vocation is only the Latin for a call.

In a celebrated passage in " Maud ", Tennyson praised the moral effects of war, and declared that some great conflict might call out the greatness even of the pacific swindlers and sweaters whom he saw around him in the commercial age. He dreamed, he said, if—

> . . . the rushing battle-bolt sang from the three-decker out of the foam,
> That the smooth-faced, snubnosed rogue would leap from his counter and till,
> And strike, if he could, were it but with his cheating yard-wand, home.

Tennyson lived in the time of a conflict more crucial and frightful than any European struggle, the conflict between the apparent artificiality of morals and the apparent immorality of science. A ship more symbolic and menacing than any foreign three-decker hove in sight in that time—the great, gory pirate-ship of Nature, challenging all the civilizations of the world. And his supreme honour is this, that he behaved like his own imaginary snubnosed rogue. His honour is that in that hour he despised the flowers and embroideries of Keats as the counter-jumper might despise his tapes and cottons. He was by nature a hedonistic and pastoral poet, but he leapt from his poetic counter and till and struck, were it but with his gimcrack mandolin, home.

Tennyson's influence on poetry may, for a time, be modified. This is the fate of every man who throws himself into his own age, catches the echo of its temporary phrases, is kept busy in battling with its temporary delusions. There are many men whom history has for a time forgotten to whom it owes more than it could count. But if Tennyson is extinguished it will be with the most glorious extinction. There are two ways in which a man may vanish—through being thoroughly conquered or through being thoroughly the Conqueror. In the main the great Broad Church philosophy which Tennyson uttered has been adopted. This will make against his fame. For a man may vanish as Chaos vanished in the face of creation, or he may vanish as God vanished in filling all things with that created life.

THE BONES OF A POEM

IT IS remarkable that Browning should have the name of an obscure and Tennyson of a lucid poet, when there are certainly passages of *In Memoriam* which are very much more difficult to understand than the mass of Browning's philosophical poetry. Browning's speech was quaint and twisted and tail foremost, but it was never vague. One of his sentences is like a dragon with his tail in his mouth; one of Tennyson's is often like a resplendent cloud that has neither head nor tail. The speaker in *Sordello* is like an excited man telling us something very important in an incomprehensible dialect. The speaker in *In Memoriam* is often like a man talking to himself about things of which we have never heard.

Properly speaking, indeed, Tennyson was more typically the poet of thought than Browning. He really attached primary importance to speculative ideas and passionless meditations upon theories about deity and immortality. In the case of Browning we feel rather that he loved a speculation as he loved a sunrise or a gallop on horseback, because it was a man's business to love as many things as he could. Browning had literally a passion about ideas; an actual human appetite. Tennyson had not a passion about ideas, he had ideas about passion. Since, therefore, *In Memoriam* has so strongly intellectual a character, a great interest attaches to attempts which have been made to detach the thread of metaphysics in it from the gorgeous and coloured threads of description and metaphor. But this is struggling with a hopeless task which would be quite simple if poetry really were what it has in most ages of classical criticism been conceived to be, a decoration or beautification of thought by simile and example. But herein has lain the great error that has much falsified criticism in this matter. Poetry is not a selection of the images which will express a particular thought; it is rather an analysis of the thoughts which are evoked by a certain image. The metaphor, the symbol, the picture, has appeared to most critics to be a mere ornament, a piece of moulding above the gateway; but it is actually the keystone of the arch. Take away the particular image employed and the whole fabric of thought falls with a crash. It is not the thought that is the deep or central thing; one might almost say that it is the phrase. In *In Memoriam*, for example, there is a description incomparably vague and perfect of the empty and idle mood often produced by sorrow:

> "The stars," she whispers, "blindly run,
> A web is wov'n across the sky;
> From out waste places comes a cry,
> And murmurs from the dying sun."

The metaphors of the passage, the stars, the web, the murmurs of the sun, are not mere illustrations, *they* are the original part of the thought. The idea of the world as a chance product has often been uttered, what is new and thrilling in the matter is the fact that the waste places and the cry of the dying sun make the idea so suddenly vivid to us that it ceases to become a thought and becomes a feeling. The phrases are strange and almost monstrous: the poet has to speak of a sun that murmurs, and a cobweb across the sky like that which the old woman swept away in the nursery rhyme. But a certain intense conception of cosmic futility was never expressed until those two or three queer words were joined together, and may never be expressed again if they are put asunder.

We may go further than this. The language of metaphysics is invariably and inevitably clumsy, because it is bound to class together moods and mental attitudes which, while they are one if expressed in terms of philosophy, would be found to be a hundred and one if they were expressed in music or landscape or literature. We speak of pessimism or idealism or a " transitory product of blind necessity " ; but when we come to actual states of feeling we find that one pessimism may differ from another as much as heaven from hell. The attitude of Walt Whitman could scarcely differ more from that of Schopenhauer than one thing that we call melancholy differs from another that we call melancholy or one thing that we call joy differs from another that we call joy. So it is with the instance from *In Memoriam* I have quoted above, which represents a frame of mind which I should not attempt to describe in prose (to do so would destroy by its own thesis), but the nature of which may be vaguely indicated by saying that it depicts a certain ghastly indolence of sorrow, an aching sterility in the hours, the sorrow of an endless afternoon.

Pessimism is not always inane and drifting, like the kind described by Tennyson ; pessimism is sometimes courageous ; strange as it may seem, it is sometimes cheerful. The good done by sceptical philosophers, indeed, has almost always resolved itself into the fact that while they were pessimists about everything else they were optimists about their own opinions : they might be living in the worst of all possible worlds, but they were the best of all possible judges of it. Between this kind of fighting inspiriting pessimism and the empty and floating kind described above in the verse from *In Memoriam*, there are innumerable shades and gradations, every one of which is a separate religion. Not only are there blue, green and crimson types both of joy and melancholy, but there is every tint of green and every tint of crimson. Yet pure verbal philosophy has no vocabulary for these degrees. It has the same word for a pessimism that drives a man to commit suicide and a pessimism that drives him to the Earls Court Exhibition. It is, as it were, still speaking of things in the gross classes of animal, vegetable and mineral, while art has found a definition for the cowslip and a worthy name for the eagle.

This is the fundamental difficulty with which the metaphysician has to contend. He tries to convey the substance of a passage by stripping away the ornaments and the verbiage, and he finds he has nothing left but the shadow. The process resembles a sort of conjuring trick in which a man should tear off the hat and coat of a man and fling them out of the window, and then discover that they remained in his hands, and it was the man that he had thrown away. For poetry is not an ornamental and indirect way of stating philosophy but a perfectly simple and direct way of stating something that is outside philosophy. There are fleeting and haphazard sights of nature that are words out of an unknown dictionary: every sunset might have founded a separate creed.

In one sense, *In Memoriam* is a work which it is especially profitable to study in detail, since not only has the whole poem a noble structure and development, but every section has a noble structure and development, and could stand, from rise to climax, as a separate poem. This unity built up of unities is one of the most perfect pieces of pure literary workmanship ever achieved. The metre, of course, is an inspiration, the two central lines falling with an almost weary harmony and the last line like an echo of something distant, a sound heard years before. Above all, it is needless to say, it is the noblest monument ever raised, a sepulchre so high as to be a cathedral for all men. And it is devoted to the expression of the most profound and stirring paradox that experience ever grew certain of, the paradox that a man can never really be miserable if he has known anything worth being miserable for. Sorrow and pessimism are by their natures opposite: sorrow rests upon the value of something; pessimism upon the value of nothing.

THE CASE FOR MACAULAY

WE HAVE all heard of prophets and poets being unpopular; and also of unpopularity as a thing that may purify the soul. But there is this further and rather odd fact—that every great man must go through a period of unpopularity, not while he is alive, but shortly after he is dead. That after eclipse is essential because in that is settled the difference between temporary and eternal oblivion. The prophet and the quack are alike admired for a generation, and admired for the wrong reasons. Then they are both forgotten, for no reason at all. But if the man is a mere quack he never returns. If he is a great man he returns, and he returns for the right reasons.

We need not dwell on the obvious instances of this. Dr. Johnson was enthroned as a cold arbiter, and dethroned as a cold arbiter. Now he has been restored as a most hot and human Christian soul, and Christians can never forget him. Dickens was adored for Little Nell, and then despised for Little Nell. It is only when Little Nell is quite dead and out of the way that he can be sufficiently adored for Dick Swiveller. Of these once popular figures there is one who has not yet recaptured his popularity. Just as a little while ago it was thought cultured to sneer at Dickens, so it is still thought cultured to sneer at Macaulay. Perhaps I had come myself to be too much under that cloud of disillusion; for when I opened Macaulay's History by accident the other day I was startled by the unmistakable roll of rich style and real greatness in the thing.

Macaulay's popularity was shallow; he was popular for the

wrong reasons. The wit of those ringing and arresting sentences is constantly coarse and unfair, though I wish it were more often remembered that this old lucid cleverness really had to be clever ; whereas our vague culture is quite free to be stupid. Wit is lower than humour ; but sham humour is much easier than sham wit. You can pretend that you have made an atmosphere ; you cannot pretend that you have made a pun. Similarly many a modern professes that his style has the nameless charm of Newman, because he could not possibly invent one clever antithesis of Macaulay. Still, Macaulay's mere wit and logic are shallow, and would not make him great. What is it, after all, that makes him great ?

This, I think, makes him great and even eternal ; that he had the high passion of history. He understood the word glory ; the glory of man as a thing like the glory of God.

The only difference between the warrior and the poet is that the warrior seeks this thing in the future and the poet or the historian in the past. Macaulay had the music of history in him, just as Walter Scott had it. He was passionately traditional. There is one unquestionable test of this : he was fond of proper names. Some of the best lines of Scott's poetry consist entirely of the names of places. Some of the strongest sentences of Macaulay hang wholly on words like Milton or Rome.

There is something that is higher than impartiality, and Macaulay possessed it ; poetical justice ; the living impartiality of the imagination rather than the dead impartiality of the reason. He sometimes made good men bad and bad men good in the heat of political prejudice ; but he always made them men, and even great men. He slandered his opponents, but he did not belittle them. He had a high pleasure in mixing with heroic affairs ; he liked to crowd his stage with men of stature and presence; he had a warlike sort of wish to see villains worthy of his heroes. Though he was not enough of a Christian to love his enemies, he was enough of a heathen to admire them; and a heathen is the next best thing. Take the case of the celebrated Graham of Claverhouse, afterwards Lord Dundee. Macaulay starts, by prejudice or purpose, indecently or even insanely against the man. He is really unreasonable in the whole affair of the Covenanters. Claverhouse, I imagine, was an ordinary officer of Dragoons, a type that does not always specialize in the Christian virtues, in the later seventeenth century, a time when the Scotch nobility and gentry were cynical and gross. It was his merely military duty to put down a rebellion of men whom you may call prophets or maniacs according to taste, but who were utterly exceptional, ruthless, and beyond common reason; who gave no quarter in battle, and wished to persecute every other religion upon earth. I daresay Claverhouse did wrong; just as any bullnecked English officer would probably do wrong in dealing with some swarm of alien fanatics. But that is all. Macaulay gives a picture of harmless and laborious peasants trampled down in blood by a monstrous fiend in top-boots, who dances on them apparently for fun. In the first few pages about John Graham, Macaulay describes a beast rather than a man. Whether he was like that in real life we need not elaborately discuss. One thing is certain: that he does not remain like that in Macaulay's History.

As soon as Dundee begins to play his great part at the very crisis of the English kingship, an extraordinary impression begins to grow. Macaulay begins to like him. Macaulay is mad for the Revolution; and he becomes quite fond of Dundee because he came so near to frustrating the Revolution. Macaulay is glad with every cell of his brain that James II should go. Yet he is thrilled through every drop of his blood when the arresting voice of Graham calls James like a trumpet to remain. When Dundee is mounted, and rides down the street, Macaulay's prose moves to the tune of Walter Scott. Stroke after stroke changes the beast to a prince of chivalry. Macaulay talks of the calm magnanimity of this monster. He goes out of his way to mention that he reproved the rapine of the clans; that he held heroic language in the council of the chiefs; and that on the eve of his last battle he asked for peril as a favour, that he might show that he was a soldier as well as a general. When the claymores come cleaving their way down Killiecrankie, Macaulay is almost a Jacobite. The last words of the great persecutor of the Covenant are lofty and unselfish; and in death he is as pure as Hector. I know no more singular change of tone in the description of one man.

This is a striking instance of what I may call the abstract enthusiasm of Macaulay. He had a passion for the cause; but he also had a passion for the subject, for the period and everybody in it. A stranger and stronger case still is that of Marlborough. If ever there was a moral dwarf, a spiritual monkey, it was he. He was a lump of littleness just large enough to be seen. He combined all despicable qualities in combinations hitherto untried. He was a thrifty profligate. He was an unpatriotic militarist. He sold his sister and his country, not madly, like a gambler, but quite quietly and explanatorily. It is almost incredible that any man, or even any animal, should be such an object of contempt. And yet Macaulay is so carried away with the great Whig Crusade, the great story that he is telling, that when dealing with one who played a large part in it, he cannot help making the man magnificent, although the part was base. He tells all the truths about Marlborough that I have cited, without the least doubt or favour; and yet he gives the impression that he has been describing a great man.

The Case for Macaulay

I have heard that somebody has started something else which is called scientific history, and I once tried to read it. It appears to avoid the dangers of describing great men by the bright and simple solution of not describing men at all. By this method the historian looks down on all the movements of men as if they were ants. If I want truth I must confess that I prefer Macaulay. I prefer to look up at men as if they were angels, even if they are angels of darkness.

LEWIS CARROLL

THE celebration of the birth of Lewis Carroll is really the celebration of the birth of Alice in Wonderland; the imaginary child being much more imaginable than the real one. Both perhaps exhibited the primness of their period; in both perhaps the primness was more formal than real. Most of us have had a glimpse, as in some stiff daguerrotype or early photograph of that epoch, of the holiday group in that sunny hour of vacation, in which a somewhat demure parson, who was a "don" or lecturer at Oxford, sat surrounded by equally demure little girls (at least in appearance) and began idly to scrawl extravagant pictures and tell a tale of topsy-turvydom apparently more crack-brained and crazy than anything that had ever been imagined in the lies of Münchausen or the lunar voyage of Ariosto. It was a new thing; Nonsense for Nonsense' sake; on the principle of art for art's sake. Nobody indeed would have been more shocked than Mr. Dodgson (which was the parson's real name) at being classed with the anarchical artists who talked about *l'art pour l'art*. But, in spite of himself, he was a much more original artist than they. He had realised that certain images and arguments could sustain themselves in the void by a sort of defiant folly; an incongruous congruity; the very aptitude of ineptitude. It was not only very new but very national. We may even say that for some time it was a secret of the English. M. Cammaerts has brilliantly described what a puzzle it appears at first to the more logical nation. It was the wild fruit of one age and people, as is proved by the fact that its only other professor, Edward Lear of the Nonsense Rhymes, was also an Englishman and also a Victorian.

Lewis Carroll

Any educated Englishman, and especially any educational Englishman (which is worse), will tell you with a certain gravity that *Alice in Wonderland* is a classic. Such is indeed the horrid truth. The original hilarity that was born on that summer afternoon among the children, in the mind of a mathematician on a holiday, has itself hardened into something almost as cold and conscientious as a holiday task. That logician's light inversion of all the standards of logic has itself, I shudder to say, stiffened into a standard work. It is a classic; that is, people praise it who have never read it. It has a secure position side by side with the works of Milton and Dryden. It is a book without which no gentleman's library is complete, and which the gentleman therefore never presumes to take out of his library. I am sorry to say it, but the soap-bubble which poor old Dodgson blew from the pipe of poetry, in a lucid interval of lunacy, and sent floating into the sky, has been robbed by educationists of much of the lightness of the bubble, and retained only the horrible healthiness of the soap.

This is not the fault of Lewis Carroll, but it is in one sense the fault of Charles Dodgson; at least the fault of the world which he inhabited and incorporated and to some extent encouraged and carried forward. His nonsense is a part of the peculiar genius of the English; but a part also of the elusive paradox of the English. None but they could have produced such nonsense; but none but they, having produced such nonsense, would ever have attempted to take it seriously. There is, by this time, a sort of implication of national loyalty about the thing; against which I for one would mildly protest. It is a moral duty to listen to reason, but it is not a moral duty to listen to unreason. It is only a lark, and no admirer of Lewis Carroll can outstrip me in liking it as a lark. As I shall suggest later, many of its really original merits as a fantasia have been missed by this heavy-handed applause; applause of work that should be criticised as it was created, with a light touch. Men may be told to listen, and in a sense even made to listen, when a man of adequate authority is talking sense. But we cannot be made to listen to a man who is talking nonsense; it sins against the whole spirit and atmosphere of the occasion, which is a holiday. Yet I have a dreadful fear that the works of Lewis Carroll are now a part of education, which in these liberal modern days means compulsory education. I once lectured before a congress of elementary schoolmasters, trying to persuade them to tolerate anything so human as Penny Dreadfuls or Dime Novels about Dick Turpin and Buffalo Bill. And I remember that the Chairman, with a refined and pained expression said, "I do not think Mr. Chesterton's brilliant paradoxes have persuaded us to put away our *Alice in Wonderland* and our"—something else, possibly *The Vicar of Wakefield* or *Pilgrim's Progress*. It never struck him that the nonsense tale is as much an escape from educational earnestness as the gallop after Buffalo Bill. For him it was simply a classic, and it went along with the other classics. And I thought to myself, with a sinking heart, "Poor, poor little Alice! She has not only been caught and made to do lessons; she has been forced to inflict lessons on others. Alice is now not only a schoolgirl but a schoolmistress. The holiday is over and Dodgson is again a don. There will be lots and lots of examination papers, with questions like: (1) What do you know of the following; mime, mimble, haddock's eyes, treacle-wells, beautiful soup? (2) Record all the moves in the chess game in *Alice Through the Looking-Glass*, and give diagram. (3) Outline the practical policy of the White Knight for dealing with the social problem of green whiskers. (4) Distinguish between Tweedledum and Tweedledee.

I will give only one deadly and devastating fact, to show how Nonsense, in the case of Alice's story, has been allowed to become cold and monumental like a classic tomb. It has been parodied. People sit down solemnly to burlesque this burlesque. They imagine they can make it funny, or at least make it funnier, by twisting its features into paltry political caricatures. They think they can give a twist, to that which has no imaginable purpose except to be twisted, by wreathing it into emblems of everyday comedy and commonplace farce. Now that is a thing that nobody would dream of doing with anything he really thought *funny*. It is only serious, and even solemn things, that can be made funny. It may be said that Sheridan burlesqued Shakespeare; at least he burlesqued the sham Shakespearean historical drama in *The Critic*. But nobody could burlesque *The Critic*. It may be said that Gilbert burlesqued Swinburne and Rossetti and all the rest of the half-pagan Pre-Raphaelites in his picture of the æsthetes in *Patience*. But no man in his senses would try to burlesque *Patience*. Nobody would think it a novelty to throw off a frivolous version of *The Bab Ballads*, and it was only an embittered enemy who uttered the celebrated sarcasm: "Why doesn't somebody bring out a comic *Punch*?" We have had Comic Histories of England and Comic Latin Grammars, because there remains a tradition that there is something serious, and even sacred, about the story of the English nation and the strong tongue of Rome. But even those who can enjoy, more than I can, what is now called a Comic Strip, would not think it a promising venture to bring out a Comic Comic Strip.

But, in the case of *Alice in Wonderland*, so strangely solid was this impression that the thing was a national institution, an educational classic, a well of English undefiled, a historic heritage like *Othello* or the *Samson Agonistes*, that satirists set seriously to work on it to make it amusing. Political parodists actually thought it a sort of improvement to give all that pure and happy pointlessness a point. They even felt, I think, a tingle of timid daring, in taking liberties with this monumental Victorian volume. They felt they were shaking the pillars of the British Constitution, when they ventured to joke about such jokes. They blasphemed the divinity of the Mock Turtle and defied the lightnings of the Mad Hatter. And each of them felt almost like a Red Republican when he took liberties with the Red Queen.

It is a delightful but difficult enterprise to liberate Lewis Carroll from the custody of Charles Dodgson. It is a hard though happy task to try to recapture the first fresh careless rapture of the days when Nonsense was new. We have to put ourselves in an utterly different attitude from that of the admirers who have come after the achievement, and feel something of the first stir and movement that went before it. In the eyes of a number of those admirers our attitude will seem like an antic, and they will be far too serious to see that it is like the original antics of Lewis Carroll. To appreciate it we must appreciate more deeply the paradox of the whole people and its literature, and the really comic contrast between its responsible and its irresponsible moods. There were a great many things that Charles Dodgson took only too seriously; but the things which his devotees have taken seriously were the things which he took lightly.

Everybody knows, I imagine, that the Rev. Charles Lutwidge Dodgson was a Fellow of Christ Church College, which nobody is allowed to call Christ Church College, but only "The House", and was a successful and even distinguished Professor of Mathematics and Logic. Superficially speaking, the most curious thing about him was that it was only through these iron gates of reason that he entered his own private paradise of unreason. All that part of the man that might have been, and in a literary man often has been, loose or light or irresponsible, was in his case particularly prim and respectable and responsible. It was only his intellect that took a holiday; his emotions never took a holiday; and certainly his conscience never took a holiday. It was perhaps a rather conventional conscience; but his moral views were quite incapable, I will not say of wavering, but even of moving or stirring; whether we class them as conventions or convictions. He had no outlet, even of imagination, on the moral or social or philosophical side: he had it only on the mathematical side. Though a conscientious mathematical teacher, he could imagine something that made plus equal to minus. But though a conscientious Christian, he could not really imagine anything that made the first last and the last first; that put down the mighty from their seat or exalted the humble and the poor. His remarks about social justice and reform, in *Sylvie and Bruno*, are more worthy of a feeble curate in a farce than of a Christian priest teaching in a historic seat of learning. He was, in the ordinary sense, limited everywhere by convention; and yet it was he who with one wild leap burst the very limits of reason. It was this stodgy and stuffy Victorian parson, who followed the wild vision of utter unreason further than it was ever pursued by any wild poet working without a conscience or an aim; by any wild painter when he dips his brush in hues of earthquake and eclipse.

The liveliest thing about him, no doubt, on the purely human side, was a real affection for children; especially for certain children. But though this was doubtless the motive that made him tell the children a story, it was not this, or anything like this, that made the story. It is a story for children, but it is not a story about children, in the same sense as the majority of children's stories. The natural extension of his imagination was all in the direction of the inverted ideas of the intellect. He could see the logical world upside down; he could not see any other kind of world even right side up. He took his triangles and turned them into toys for a favourite little girl; he took his logarithms and syllogisms and twisted them into nonsense. But, in a rather special sense, there is nothing but nonsense in his nonsense. There is no sense in his nonsense; as there is in the more human nonsense of Rabelais or the more bitter nonsense of Swift. If he had been suggesting any moral or metaphysical ideas, they would never have been so deep or grand as those of Rabelais or Swift. But he was only playing The Game of Logic; and it is his glory that it was a new game, and a nonsensical game, and one of the best games in the world.

Nevertheless, in a certain subconscious world of the English spirit, of his whole home and tradition and ancestry, there is something rather deeper than this. There was something that a man must perhaps be an Englishman to understand; something perhaps that he must even have been a Victorian to understand; something, after all, that he must perhaps reconcile himself to enjoy and not understand. It works back to that word "holiday", that I have used several times in this connection, and which is really the key of the problem. There is a sense in which a man like Rabelais was not really on a holiday. He really was building The Abbey of Theleme, however fantastically and with whatever wild gargoyles or toppling spires. In every sense we may say that Mr. Lemuel Gulliver, when he went on his travels, was not going merely on his holidays. These writers had a purpose, and it was, whatever its defects, very largely the serious intellectual purpose of their lives. But the strange nation of the English, in their strange phase of Victorianism, had something much more subtle about their ideas of business and pleasure; and the pure nonsense they invented really was a holiday of the mind. I have said that it was an original thing, and it was; one of the few things, like Gothic architecture, that had really never been done before. It was something to invent a happy nightmare; it was something more to create a thing that was at once lawless and innocent. It was a sort of dream-life, lived by the nineteenth-century Englishman parallel to his rather too realistic real life. It had something of Dual Personality, though without any savour of diabolic possession. It had a suggestion of living a double life; though without anything of the mortal moral issue of Jekyll and Hyde. Dr. Jekyll tried to perform a surgical operation to remove his conscience; Mr. Dodgson only amputated his common sense. It was his head, and not his heart, that he detached and sent adrift like a bubble in a world of merely abstract anarchy. And in this he discovered some secret in the mind of the modern Englishman, which has given the story and the style a secure position; even, as has been hinted, a position almost too secure. It was the avowal of a sport or enjoyment to which the whole mind of the people must have been already tending. Perhaps it was not for nothing that one of the comic artists of *Punch* wrote a serious novel, about a man who lived a continuous dreaming life, side by side with his waking life. The Victorian Englishman walked the world in broad daylight, a proverbially solid figure, with his chimney-pot hat and his mutton-chop whiskers, with his business bag and his business-like umbrella. But something happened to him at night; some wind of nightmare blowing through his soul and his subconsciousness dragged him out of bed and whirled him out of the window, where he rose into a world of wind and moonshine; his chimney-pot hat sailing high above the chimneys and his umbrella bellying like a balloon or bearing him upwards like a witch's broom; with his whiskers waving like wings.

HOW PLEASANT TO KNOW MR. LEAR

MANY who remember the admirable poem in which Mr. Edward Lear professed to describe his own personality will probably prefer it to a longer account of him in prose. It is not supremely important to know where Edward Lear was born, or what were his views on politics; but the information conveyed in the line—

> He weareth a runcible hat

is really solid and important. It was also essential to appreciate the distinction involved in the words—

> He reads, but he cannot speak Spanish,
> He cannot abide Ginger Beer.

And, after reading the poem, we were all quite ready to agree in concluding the verse :—

> Ere the days of his pilgrimage vanish
> How pleasant to know Mr. Lear.

I, for one, am prepared to believe in the eternal and spiritual Edward Lear against all shows of this world and all phantoms of the flesh. I believe that " his body *was* perfectly spherical ", and that he did verily and in truth wear a runcible hat. I will have no Modernism on this subject; or indeed on any other. Perhaps there was a sensible Edward Lear who wrote letters and criticised current affairs. But the great Edward Lear, the serious Edward Lear, was the silly one.

It is a remarkable fact that the two great English masters

of nonsense in the nineteenth century were both men whose private personalities were, I will not say prosaic, but at least rational, respectable, and containing no suggestion at all either of pure poetry or of any particular oddity in humour. Lewis Carroll and Edward Lear were neither of them really people with perverse or whimsical temperaments; they were neither of them men like Charles Lamb or Robert Louis Stevenson, men who could not write ten words on a postcard without the sentence taking a sort of tender twist. The views of Edward Lear, like those of the respected don who wrote under the name of Lewis Carroll, were sensible and slightly Philistine views. It would immediately be supposed that this sane but stolid character would be somewhat unsuited for two wild poets, who were to write about the Jabberwock and the Dong with the Luminous Nose. I am not so sure that this is really the case. I go so far as to say that the solid mid-Victorian lives led by Lewis Carroll and Edward Lear had a great deal to do with their creating themselves kings of the remote empire of unreason. The simplicity and rationality of that race attracted the fairies. They had a basis, moral and material, on which the bizarre pagodas could be built. It is too little remembered that if you want to reach nonsense you must go through sense.

Of course there was a difference of degree in the two cases and even, perhaps, a difference of kind. Edward Lear in his letters is not subtle, but he is exhilarating. Mr. Dodgson, in his private utterances, was neither exhilarating nor subtle. But they were both very good examples of the well-informed Englishman of the mid-Victorian time. And the chief mark of the well-informed Englishman of that time was that he was an ill-informed Englishman. It is impossible to read Lear's letters without feeling how insulated and provincial were the best English minds during a certain period. Here is a man of genius, a good Greek scholar, a traveller of experience, a man priding himself on the liberality of his mind; and yet he criticises all things not English as if they were indefensible eccentricities in an English village. He has the typical mid-Victorian habit of getting horribly angry with the tyrants or impostors who are not oppressing him, but being perfectly genial and self-satisfied about those who really are. He breaks out, as Thackeray did, into pages of denunciation of the life of a monastery; though he does not (as Thackeray did) actually propose that monastic vows should be legally forbidden, like human sacrifice. But he does fly into a furious and sustained passion against a system which is, after all, a voluntary system, while it never occurs to him to make any protest against the dominance of the English aristocracy, which is not voluntary—except on the part of the aristocrats. A few poor old monks who have chosen to live hard lives on their own responsibility strike him as monsters of darkness and hypocrisy. "I still maintain that Blasphemy and lying are the Prerogatives of Priestcraft." But when he comes to a quite typical diplomatist and cynical oligarch like Lord Palmerston, that statesman's front bench clap-trap strikes him as "all straightforward bluff truth". Like all the English of his strange time he could have seen that the Irish were a priest-led people; but could not have seen that the English are a squire-led people. And it is surely more manly to follow the leaders of your own philosophy than merely to follow the owners of your own farms. Such are at least the letters of Edward Lear; full of broad English fun, full of splendid English high spirits. But the very broadness of the fun only illustrates the narrowness of the outlook. Even the high spirits only show the low political education. Everything that is English is liberal; especially the illiberal aristocracy. Everything that is un-English is illiberal, especially the tradition which has been the mother of all the liberal arts. Nobody wants him to go into a monastery ; yet he will soothe his soul with incessant roarings against the hocus-pocus of monasteries. As if all the hocus-pocus of all the priests in history could really be much more dangerous than the hocus-pocus of Lord Palmerston.

To say this is of course to leave out of the real Edward Lear a great mass of real humour, of real liberality, and knowledge of the world. Nevertheless, if we drop the real Edward Lear and turn to the unreal one—oh, bless him, how much more real he is ! The mystical Edward Lear, the one who wore the runcible hat, is one of the great masters of English literature. He has, no doubt, essential points in common with his mere earthly counterpart. When we read those criticisms of Continental religion mentioned above, we may perhaps see a deep truth in the line—

He reads, but he cannot speak Spanish.

That was really what was the matter with the Englishman of the Lear period ; he could read about foreigners, but he could not speak with them. And when we delight (as we certainly do when reading his letters) in the heartiness, the good fellowship, the Dickensian camaraderie of that fine old English world, we may add with enthusiasm the line, as if we were shouting it all together in a chorus—

He cannot *abide* Ginger Beer !

But the Lear of the nonsense world still remains a sort of super-Lear, a being far more transcendental and awful.

For the truth is that Edward Lear was greater than Lewis Carroll ; at least, he could do what Lewis Carroll could not do. Lewis Carroll's nonsense was merely mathematical and logical. Edward Lear's nonsense was emotional and poetical. The long rolling lines of Lear have the feeling of fine poetry in them, which does not exist in the excellent poem of " Jabberwocky ". It does exist in

> Far and few, far and few,
> Are the lands where the Jumblies live

or in those splendid lines—

> When awful darkness and silence reign
> Over the great Gromboolian plain,
> Through the long, long wintry nights ;—
> When the angry breakers roar
> As they beat on the rocky shore ;—
> When Storm-clouds brood on the towering heights
> Of the Hills of the Chankly Bore.

No one was ever quite at home in Wonderland—not even Alice. But the English romanticism in those lines of Lear is so strong that I feel as if the Chankly Bore were in Berkshire or Sussex, and I know I am native to the Gromboolian Plain.

THE GENIUS OF GILBERT

AN EDITION of "Her Majesty's Ship Pinafore" in a prose form with pictures is presumably meant strictly for the nursery; and in such a light it is excellent, first because of the genuine excellence of the pictures, and second because there is something in Sir William Gilbert's fancy which pleases children, though it certainly was not meant for them. It is an awful rebuke for the satirist that children enjoy his work without seeing the satire. That harsh outline and emphatic colour which for us makes a caricature cruel, for a child only makes it clear. Swift created *Gulliver* as a cataract of contempt for the children of men. And the children of men have drunk it delightedly and washed in it innocently ever since. Swift described his giants and pigmies in order to show how vile and vain a world it is in which everything is at the mercy of relativity. But the child reading Swift merely thinks how living and lovely a world it is, in which there are giants and pigmies at all. Much in the same way there must be many people (I am one of them) who owe their first primitive poetic impression of a modern English ship to the preposterous ship "Pinafore". I actually received the whole naval romance from this fantasia, which had no apparent object except to make game of the whole naval romance. The clean look of a deck, the smartness of the white sailors, the cocked hat and strict blue uniform of a captain, all these picturesque images I saw while sitting, as a small boy, in the pit of the theatre, long before I saw them anywhere else. As I was an English school-boy, it is as needless to say that I was taught no English History during the term as to say that I was taken to "Pinafore" during the holidays. That is the way we do things; and there may be something in it. But certainly I saw the great satire on the national navy long before I saw the national navy, or had even, in any serious sense, heard of it. I knew all the ropes and the rig of "H.M.S. Pinafore" before I had counted the masts of any craft to be seen at Margate; that caricatured and comic ship was really (in the words of its own satiric verse) the only ship I had ever seen. I knew something of the routine of sailors and the position of the quarter deck before I had seen the harbour of Portsmouth, or the spot where Nelson fell.

This is no doubt the justification of such a simplified and illustrated reproduction of the thing for children. Nevertheless it cannot be regarded as other than an inversion of the proper state of affairs. It is wrong that children should complete their own excellent common sense by staring at the mature madness of their elders. It is unreasonable that a child should never have heard of tea until he reads about the Mad Hatter's tea-party. It is wrong that he should never have heard of babies until he has read *The Water Babies.* Some more simple and solid picture of this earth as it is will always delight children, and ought to be prepared and preserved for them. Sense is the suitable atmosphere of children, because they never get tired of it. Nonsense is a playground for grown-up people; and I, for one, object to a lot of officious children coming and interfering with my play.

At any rate, the true genius of Gilbert is at the opposite extreme to the genius of childhood. The magic of a man like Gilbert is that he can see things just slightly crooked; the magic of a child is that he sees things startlingly and almost shockingly straight. Both bear witness to truth; but the humorist bears witness by exaggerating, the child by not exaggerating at all. I give the nearest example I have known.

A little boy was sitting on my knee the other day while I was reading a new book of philosophy. He could just read capital letters, and he read across the top of a chapter " What is truth ?" And the moment he saw this grey and ironical riddle of old Pontius Pilate, he called out in a sudden shrill and exultant voice, " Oh, that *is* an easy question. I know what truth is. It's saying things right." And so indeed it is ; that is the best answer to the question, except the colossal silence of Christ. But the point is here, that the whole strength of the child lay not in the fact that he solved the difficulty, but that he did not admit that there was any difficulty. That is really to be close to God. But the whole point of humour in the Gilbertian sense is that it does see the difficulty, that it sees innumerable difficulties arising out of the difficulty, and that by turning the riddle back upon itself, it comes back to common sense. Compare with the boy's boisterous disdain for so simple a problem as that of truth, the treatment of the same thing in the "Mikado". Modern philosophers and psychologists (being by no means near to God) have started all sorts of fads about truthfulness ; and one of them is this : that certain people (Teutons especially) are so splendidly strong and brave that truth comes out of them naturally and is part of their animal dignity and simplicity. Of course, every child knows that this is nonsense ; every child (Teutonic or otherwise) knows that it is nice to tell a lie, but that by a considerable effort one can tell the truth. But the philosophers do suggest that there is a truth-telling type, a person to whom deception is instinctively painful. Gilbert, the great satirist of our subtleties, seizes hold of this particular subtlety and smashes it for ever in four ironical lines.

We know him well, he cannot tell
Untrue or groundless tales,

He always tries to utter lies
And every time he fails.

That is the summary of the supreme inspiration of Gilbert; to take some nonsense that is said everywhere; and to say it so nonsensically that no one can ever say it again.

In all this, Gilbert was very much the precursor and even the anticipator of Mr. Bernard Shaw. He had the power of putting a prejudice suddenly under a light in which it could not live. He performed the true purpose of a plague or a consuming fire; he burnt up everything that can be burnt. For instance, the real idea of patriotism cannot be burnt; it is incombustible and incorrupt. Whatever anyone says, it is true that Frenchmen not only live in France, but live by France. Whatever anyone says, where two or three Frenchmen are gathered together, France shall be in the midst of them. But there is an element in patriotism, especially, I am afraid, in English patriotism, which invites a slaughterous scientific attack. It has invited it, and it has got it. A number of young Englishmen have obviously got into their minds the extraordinary notion that the greatness of England ought to make an Englishman proud. The truth is just the reverse, the greatness of England ought to make an Englishman humble. One ought not to swagger about being the fellow citizen of Shakespeare; rather one ought to feel that Shakespeare might have had a better fellow citizen. In other words, an Englishman ought to feel unworthy of his country; it is only fools or aliens who feel worthy of it. But there does exist this false patriotism which is not so much love of England as pleasure in being an Englishman. I say it does exist; but its back has been broken with a blow. Gilbert has in one phrase defined and destroyed it. In the moment when Gilbert wrote the lines

But in spite of all temptations
To belong to other nations
He remains an Englishman——

in that hour he effaced the folly of making national peculiarities a ground of spiritual pride.

THE STYLE OF NEWMAN

A FINE style is not a narrow or fastidious or aristocratic thing, as many think. On the contrary, style is the truly democratic thing, since it touches all common things with the same fairy wand. A man who loves all men enough to use them rightly is a democrat. A man who loves all words enough to use them rightly is a stylist. Style comes out, as the fraternal human sentiment comes out, pre-eminently and most definitely in dealing with coarse or everyday things. An eloquent outburst from Carlyle about the stars and the heroes is, in its own way, fine style. But a page of Newman's *Apologia* which merely describes how he left off living at some college and went to live in some settlement is also fine style. The ideal lover of mankind would linger over a postcard to his washerwoman, transposing words and modifying adjectives until it was as perfect as a sonnet.

The one weakness of Newman's temper and attitude as a whole was, I think, that he lacked the democratic warmth. This had nothing to do with his religion ; for in Manning, who was a far more rigid and central Catholic than he, democracy roared like a bonfire. It had something to do with his character and something to do with his training. But in this matter of a fine style Newman was not doing anything precious or exclusive ; he was doing something entirely human and sociable. Good style treats verbs and particles as good manners treats chairs and tables, easily but in the proper way. There is no such thing as being a gentleman at important moments ; it is at unimportant moments that a man is a gentleman. At important moments he ought to be something better. So while we can consent to receive some poignant message or violent and sudden sincerity in any language that the man chooses to use, we feel that the finest instinct of geniality is to speak of common things with some dignity and care. No man has ever done this so well as Newman. A magic that is like a sort of musical accompaniment changes and heightens the most prosaic fragments of personal biography or scholastic explanation. And in this, as I say, he achieves for a time that awful and beautiful thing which is the dream of all democracy, the seeing of all things as wonderful, the thing for which Whitman strove and which he did not perfectly attain. In this respect Carlyle and Walt Whitman (that immeasurably greater man) are even the aristocrats compared to this classical embroiderer. They spoke in a tongue not understanded of the people. They were bold and boisterous and personal, as the better kind of aristocrats are always bold and boisterous and personal.

There is another element in Newman's style which is worth noticing as a guide for all controversialists. He had the same knack in discussion which Gladstone had, the air of not being in any way in a hurry. Young men who read Gladstone's speeches in printed books just after his career had closed in unpopularity often could not see wherein lay the overwhelming witchcraft which made vast audiences rise like one man and vast combinations follow the orator to defeat. The oratorical style seemed to them wordy and winding, full of endless parentheses and needless distinctions. The truth is, I imagine, that it was precisely the air of leisure and large-mindedness, this scrupulosity about exceptions, this allowance for misunderstandings, that gave to the final assertion its sudden fire. Both Newman and Gladstone often seemed, in their mildness and restraint, a long time coming to the point, but the point was deadly sharp. This is very much mirrored in their style. Both men had one particularly rhetorical effect perfectly : the art of passing smoothly and yet suddenly from philosophical to popular language. A hundred examples or parallels might be given if I had all their works before me : one parallel, which I happen to remember, may suffice. Gladstone, in answering one of the early Unionist orators who had appealed to the idea that all the intellectual people were Unionist, very gently deprecated this mode of argument. He asked his hearers (I have forgotten the words, but there were a great many of them and they were very long ones) to confess, if necessary, that they were the inferiors of their opponents in erudition, in opportunities, in culture. " So that nothing remains for us," he said, " but to show that we have better *manners* "—and the sudden stress on the word must have been like a blow. Almost exactly the same kind of abrupt colloquialism marks the wonderful termination of the introduction to the *Apologia*. With careful and melancholy phrases Newman describes how delicate and painful a matter it must necessarily be to give an account to the world of all the secret transitions of the soul. " But I do not like to be called a knave and liar to my face, and———" The dramatic effect is almost exactly the same. It is, indeed, a rather singular fact that although Newman's style is so harmonious and limpid, yet the peculiar force of that style generally consists in its use for sharply different purposes. Nobody, I imagine, who has read the *Apologia* will ever forget that transition, which strikes the reader not only as thrilling but almost as queer, in the passage dealing with his first relations with Edgbaston. He describes, in quiet detail, how he went to this place and that place ; how he was, in consequence, asked this and that question ; how his opponents could not explain legitimately his reason for leaving on such and such a day or going to such and such a destination ; how they plied him with questions and haunted him with suggestions. Then he turns and calls them, with a cry like thunder, "Cowards." "It is not you," he says, "that I fear; it is not you from whom I am hiding, *Di me terrent et Jupiter hostis.*"

The truth was, as I fancy, that it was very fortunate for Newman, considered merely as a temperament and a personality, that he was forced into that insatiably fighting thing, the Catholic Church, and that he was forced into it in a deeply Protestant country. His spirit might have been too much protected by the politeness of our English temper and our modern age, but it was flayed alive by the living spirit of "No Popery". The frigid philosopher was called a liar and turned into a man. We might also dwell upon that one outburst of wild and exuberant satire in which Newman indulged: I mean his comparison (in the first lecture on "The Position of English Catholics") of the English view of the Catholic Church to the probable Russian view of the British Constitution. It is one of the great pages of fierce English humour. Why he thus once exploded into fantastic derision I do not know. But I suspect that it was because Birmingham was full of "No Popery" rioters and his back was to the wall. This man, when he was in the sweet but too refined atmosphere of the Oxford High Churchmen, had shed many tears. But, like all brave men when he first saw the face of battle, he began to laugh.

IBSEN

I

IBSEN belongs to a certain group which it is a delicate point to define. To call them the great Provincials may be mistaken for offensive patronage ; but surely all will agree that it is less offensive to call men Provincial than to call them Nordic. God forbid that we should say that Ibsen was Nordic ; but it was not an accident that he was Norwegian. The point about the group is this : that they were men thinking for themselves, but largely cut off from the old thought of the world ; by an accidental barrier of recent revolts and negations in the North. A Catholic naturally feels this, especially in their exile from Catholicism ; but it is true of much else, as generally of Classicism. It meant an under-estimate of Aristotle as well as of Aquinas. It knew too little of the vine and olive as well as of the bread and wine. It was not rebelling against these ancient things, but entirely against the modern things that had been built to block them out ; the Victorian comfort and convention. And these nobler barbarians, remote from Rome, were sometimes so ignorant that they did not know when they were Roman—or when they were right.

When popular tradition resists by instinct some crude or questionable novelty, it has a curious way of giving the wrong reason even for doing the right thing. When the Victorian Philistine first grumbled at Ibsen, he always had the tone of saying, " Oh, I daresay all this dismal pessimism may be very deep and philosophical ; but I don't go to the theatre for philosophy ; I like a play to be a play, and have a plot, and be about ordinary jolly people." Now in fact that criticism allows far too much to Ibsen, while it also grants him too little. The solid merits by which Ibsen really won his way were, first, that he had a highly original but a highly practical and effective stage-craft; and sense of a play as a play. And, second, that he was interested in real human beings; and in the curious clashes and deadlocks that do really happen in parlours and dining-rooms. His philosophy, as philosophy, was generally extremely poor. His thinking about abstract things was often strangely thin and shallow. It was he, I think, who coined the phrase: "How do we know that two and two do not make five in the fixed stars?" to which the obvious answer is: "At least as well as we know there are any fixed stars." The very distinction between fixed and unfixed stars is only established by pages of mathematics; or, in other words, by assuming about two thousand times over that two and two do not make five. That there is a mental limit in man, at which mathematics also become mysteries, is quite true; but it has nothing to do with a vulgar test of locality; and the riddle is not found in the Pleiades at a certain distance from the earth, any more than it is in the earth at a certain distance from the Pleiades. It is as if a man were to say, "I have never been in Upper Norwood; so existence and non-existence may be the same in that suburb." If we were to attempt to state Ibsen in mere terms of thought, especially of what is called free thought, we should find ourselves dealing with a great deal of this very thoughtless thought. It is not even pessimism; it is rather that sort of bewildered optimism which is so often left in vague minds by the frustration of an impossible freedom. When the soul has wandered among all the wandering stars, without finding one of them in which four is the same as five, it can only come home again with a dazed expression; and that is often the end of Ibsen, considered as a thinker. But there is a great deal more to be said about Ibsen considered as a creator. The moment he is content to be a craftsman, and express himself through the images of his craft, he expresses living truths too great to be defined by the craftsman, let alone critic. Pessimism is nonsense; but the sullen energy of Borkman is not nonsense. Optimism is nonsense; but the innocent violence of the Enemy of the People is not nonsense. Hedda Gabler is a very unpleasant person; but, to do her justice, she is not an "ism." In other words, she is not a heresy; an infectious disease of the intellect. Ibsen's work had certain elements of imaginative truth, which overcame all the intellectual falsehood implied in being "modern." And when he thus trusted his imagination, it is curious to note how near he was to much older things than the nineteenth century. He was really in revolt against the nineteenth century; just as his doctor was in revolt against its "compact liberal majority."

Thus, the Master Builder is as medieval as his name. He is all the more medieval for not knowing it. For the chief charm of medieval people was that they never thought about being medieval. It is the chief inferiority of modern people that they do think about being modern. But not only does his very title imply the old conception of a craft, the real moral of the tragedy is the noble conception of the responsibility of the craftsman. It really is the great modern immorality that builders cannot climb their own towers; that men do not see the end of their own work; that an indirect and servile complexity has excused the shop-keeper from living over his shop or the captain from going down in his ship. Men make machines larger than they can control, as Ibsen's hero made a tower higher than he could climb. Men grow dizzy with their own civilization, as he grew giddy on his own spire. Probably Ibsen would have defined it very imperfectly as an idea; but he made it immortal as an image.

II

The great dramatist Ibsen will certainly be of enduring interest as a dramatist; he will also be of enduring interest as the symbol of the very strange period through which we have just passed. That period is very hard to describe. It was the period during which the great European effort to break down inequality itself broke down. Before Democracy had become successful it had become old-fashioned. Just as the dogmas of Republicanism were triumphing over the dogmas of Oligarchy, the world suddenly wearied of both dogmas alike. There ensued an extraordinary period in which most men of my generation or of any approximate generation grew up; a period in which the dogmas of Democracy, being the most historically immediate, were felt to be the most dogmatic, and therefore the most irritating. Because they were the newest dogmas, men felt them to be the most antiquated dogmas. During this period the one thing that seemed far off and feeble and almost legendary was the austere humanitarianism, the stern humanitarianism of the French Revolution. During this period the one thing that was felt to be wrong was the conception of the rights of man.

But there were in this strange and empty epoch another class of men, a class of men really great and serious, who were superior to all these things. They saw that the breakdown of the pure democratic doctrine was but a symbol of the breakdown of all doctrines. They said that a man must be free as regards his individuality, not merely as regards his citizenship. Democracy declares that a man should have liberty indeed, but should have that liberty which other men have. This school felt that the particular liberty which a man should above all things have, was the liberty which other men did not have. Their individual aimed not merely at being free, but at being unique, indeed, at being solitary. They set the claims of men against the rights of men. Of these there were many brilliant and base within the period of the last fifty years. Of these the greatest was Ibsen.

He made no disguise of being in ethics merely a gigantic opportunist. He made no disguise at all of his passionate hatred of Democracy. In the old epic or legend of nineteenth-century reform the hero was the People. Ibsen's hero was the Enemy of the People. He did not use that phrase in irony; he deliberately made Dr. Stockmann at the very beginning of his remarks, and before anyone worth mentioning has attacked him at all, deliver a wild and whirling defence of aristocracy, full of the suggestion that the minority is always right and the majority always wrong. Ibsen himself was in spirit and essence always the enemy of the people; far more the enemy of the people than poor Nietzsche. To this day those few of the real people who have heard his name hate it.

In all this he was sincere beyond the point of sublimity. He had the largest kind of courage and what commonly goes with courage—simplicity. I cannot understand those who regard him as a mere artist. He seems to me to be as fierce as Mr. Bernard Shaw upon his own dogma. Only, as in the case of Mr. Bernard Shaw, his dogma is that there is no dogma. It is quite true, as so many of his critics have said, that he writes one play against one doctrine and then another play against the opposite doctrine. It is quite true that in the "Enemy of the People" he attacks the ideal of decorous silence, and that in "The Wild Duck" he attacks the ideal of indecorous candour. But this is because what he wants to attack in both cases is ideals. He is not really angry with the ideal of silence or with the ideal of candour; he is angry with the ideal of idealism. And in this he seems to me to have been always splendidly consistent, splendidly fierce, splendidly wrong.

His dislike of idealism would alone separate him from the populace and the popular theory of government, for the populace is always idealistic. But there is here a deeper matter also. The whole of that problem play which will be always associated with his name is a thing profoundly plutocratic. The whole of the modern attack upon marriage and the family is in its inmost nature plutocratic. In every problem play that ever I saw or heard of there was one assumption—that all the people in it had plenty of money. And the necessity of this is obvious. In the majority of sane human lives there is no problem of sex at all; there is no problem of marriage at all; there is no problem of temperament at all; for all these problems are dwarfed and rendered ridiculous by the standing problem of being a moderately honest man and paying the butcher. The philosophical upshot of most problem plays is practically this, that if two married people moon about in large rooms all day long, it is highly probable that they will get on each other's nerves. On this basis (a purely plutocratic basis) a large number of modern people have erected an attack upon monogamy; saying that it is not good for two people to be always together. The only weakness in the argument is that in actual human monogamy the two people are not always together. Both the man and the woman have apart from each other an exceedingly hard time. We read poems and legends of parted lovers. Why, half the affectionate married couples of the world are perpetually parted lovers. An omnibus conductor and his wife see almost as little of each other as Romeo and Juliet. A postman and his chosen meet if not secretly, at least by night. Hence follows the fact that none of our intellectuals can understand ; that the actual emotions of the democracy are much simpler and younger and more straightforward than those of a more fortunate class. A very hard-working man cannot get tired of his family. A very hard-working man can hardly get used to them.

But this is a truth which literally cannot be expressed in any drama, however realistic. For this purpose the closest realism is as useless as the wildest sentimentalism. Ibsen brought to the most astonishing perfection the technical talent of reality ; and he has had many imitators more realistic, if less inspired. We can have in our plays the realism of the man who turns up his trousers before going out at the back door. We can have in our plays the realism of the man who goes out at the back door and then comes back for his umbrella. But there is one thing that no realist, however daring, however frantic, would venture to depict upon the stage. He may make indecencies walk naked in the open day. He may cry from the housetops the things of shame which humanity has kept secret for centuries. But there is one thing that no dramatist dare produce upon the stage. That thing is the thing called " Work." There is no playwright who would reproduce upon the stage the first four hours of an ordinary clerk's day. Nobody would send up the curtain at 8 o'clock on a man adding up figures, and send it down at 10 o'clock on a man still adding up figures. Even an Ibsenite audience would not support the silent symbolism of three scenes all of which were occupied with the same bricklayer laying bricks. We dare not say in artistic form how much there is of prose in men's lives ; and precisely because we cannot say how much there is of prose, we cannot say how much there is of poetry. It was not merely that Ibsen was not enough of a democrat to understand and respect marriage. It was also that Ibsen was not enough of a realist to understand and respect marriage.

Marriage and the family fidelity are essential and sacred things, exactly for those reasons that cannot be adequately expressed in art at all; for all art is a thing of glimpses, and marriage is a thing of continuity. Dramas, however realistic, deal with events. But monogamy is not merely a good event; it is a good habit. Ibsen was a very great man who made art as realistic as it can well be; it cannot be entirely realistic. But if it were entirely realistic, it would be almost entirely romantic.

I do not take the view that Ibsen was a mere iconoclast by temperament and desire. I believe that he would, like most men of his time, have been sincerely glad to have possessed a positive philosophy; I believe he did not possess it, and I believe he was a profoundly unhappy man. It is true that he admired youth and its beautiful energy, as in Hilda Wangel.

But then people who can believe in nothing else always do believe in that; the last statues that the Romans made were the statues of young barbarians. It is true, and it is a merit of his, far too little admired by his admirers, that he had a vast amount of poetry in his composition and that he reminds one constantly of northern folk-lore and fairy-tales. Ibsen is much more like Hans Andersen than he is like any English writer. The man with the strange eyes in the "Lady from the Sea," the Rat Wife in "Little Eyolf," the queer business of the bird in the "Wild Duck," the queer business of the tower in the "Master Builder"—all those things are very full of mysticism. No one wishes to underrate Ibsen so far as to deny that he was a mystic. But all this does not affect the question of Ibsen's positive belief about things; it does not show that Ibsen had any religion. It only shows that Ibsen had plenty of superstition, which in the case of so sensible a man might be taken for granted. Religion is a rare and definite conviction of what this world of ours really is. Superstition is only the commonsense acceptation of what it obviously is. Sane peasants, healthy hunters, are all superstitious; they are superstitious because they are healthy and sane. They have a reasonable fear of the unknown; for superstition is only the creative side of agnosticism. The superstitious man sees quite plainly that the universe is a thing to be feared. The religious man maintains paradoxically that the universe is a thing to be trusted. The awe is certainly the obvious thing; the fear of the Lord is the beginning of wisdom; and no one denies that Ibsen and the savages have begun to be wise. The fear of the Lord is the beginning of wisdom—but not the end.

OSCAR WILDE

THE time has certainly come when this extraordinary man, Oscar Wilde, may be considered merely as a man of letters. He sometimes pretended that art was more important than morality, but that was mere play-acting. Morality or immorality was more important than art to him and everyone else. But the very cloud of tragedy that rested on his career makes it easier to treat him as a mere artist now. His was a complete life, in that awful sense in which your life and mine are incomplete; since we have not yet paid for our sins. In that sense one might call it a perfect life, as one speaks of a perfect equation; it cancels out. On the one hand we have the healthy horror of the evil; on the other the healthy horror of the punishment. We have it all the more because both sin and punishment were highly civilized; that is, nameless and secret. Some have said that Wilde was sacrificed; let it be enough for us to insist on the literal meaning of the word. Any ox that is really sacrificed is made sacred.

But the very fact that monstrous wrong and monstrous revenge cancel each other, actually does leave this individual artist in that very airy detachment which he professed to desire. We can really consider him solely as a man of letters.

About Oscar Wilde, as about other wits, Disraeli or Bernard Shaw, men wage a war of words, some calling him a great artist and others a mere charlatan. But this controversy misses the really extraordinary thing about Wilde: the thing that appears rather in the plays than the poems. He was a great artist. He also was really a charlatan. I mean by a charlatan one sufficiently dignified to despise the tricks that he employs.

A vulgar demagogue is not a charlatan; he is as coarse as his crowd. He may be lying in every word, but he is sincere in his style. Style (as Wilde might have said) is only another name for spirit. Again, a man like Mr. Bernard Shaw is not a charlatan. I can understand people thinking his remarks hurried or shallow or senselessly perverse, or blasphemous, or merely narrow. But I cannot understand anyone failing to feel that Mr. Shaw is being as suggestive as he can, is giving his brightest and boldest speculations to the rabble, is offering something which he honestly thinks valuable. Now Wilde often uttered remarks which he must have known to be literally valueless. Shaw may be high or low, but he never talks down to the audience. Wilde did talk down, sometimes very far down.

Wilde and his school professed to stand as solitary artistic souls apart from the public. They professed to scorn the middle class, and declared that the artist must not work for the bourgeois. The truth is that no artist so really great ever worked so much for the bourgeois as Oscar Wilde. No man, so capable of thinking about truth and beauty, ever thought so constantly about his own effect on the middle classes. He studied them with exquisite attention, and knew exactly how to shock and how to please them. Mr. Shaw often gets above them in seraphic indignation, and often below them in sterile and materialistic explanations. He disgusts them with new truths or he bores them with old truths; but they are always living truths to Bernard Shaw. Wilde knew how to say the precise thing which, whether true or false, is irresistible. As, for example, "I can resist everything but temptation."

But he sometimes sank lower. One might go through his swift and sparkling plays with a red and blue pencil marking two kinds of epigrams; the real epigram which he wrote to please his own wild intellect, and the sham epigram which he wrote to thrill the very tamest part of our tame civilization. This is what I mean by saying that he was strictly a charlatan—among other things. He descended below himself to be on top of others. He became purposely stupider than Oscar Wilde that he might seem cleverer than the nearest curate. He lowered himself to superiority; he stooped to conquer.

One might easily take examples of the phrase meant to lightly touch the truth and the phrase meant only to bluff the bourgeoisie. For instance, in "A Woman of No Importance," he makes his chief philosopher say that all thought is immoral, being essentially destructive; "Nothing survives being thought of." That is nonsense, but nonsense of the nobler sort; there is an idea in it. It is, like most professedly modern ideas, a death-dealing idea not a life-giving one; but it is an idea. There is truly a sense in which all definition is deletion. Turn a few pages of the same play and you will find somebody asking, "What is an immoral woman?" The philosopher answers, "The kind of woman a man never gets tired of." Now that is not nonsense, but rather rubbish. It is without value of any sort or kind. It is not symbolically true; it is not fantastically true; it is not true at all.

Anyone with the mildest knowledge of the world knows that nobody can be such a consuming bore as a certain kind of immoral woman. That vice never tires men, might be a tenable and entertaining lie; that the individual instrument of vice never tires them is not, even as a lie, tenable enough to be entertaining. Here the great wit was playing the cheap dandy to the incredibly innocent; as much as if he had put on paper cuffs and collars. He is simply shocking a tame curate; and he must be rather a specially tame curate even to be shocked. This irritating duplication of real brilliancy with snobbish bluff runs through all his three comedies. "Life is much too important to be taken seriously"; that is the true humorist. " A well-tied tie is the first serious step in life " ; that is the charlatan. " Man can believe the impossible, but man can never believe the improbable " ; that is said by a fine philosopher. " Nothing is so fatal to a personality as the keeping of promises, unless it be telling the truth " ; that is said by a tired quack. " A man can be happy with any woman so long as he does not love her " ; that is wild truth. " Good intentions are invariably ungrammatical " ; that is tame trash.

But while he had a strain of humbug in him, which there is not in the demagogues of wit like Bernard Shaw, he had, in his own strange way, a much deeper and more spiritual nature than they. Queerly enough, it was the very multitude of his falsities that prevented him from being entirely false. Like a many-coloured humming top, he was at once a bewilderment and a balance. He was so fond of being many-sided that among his sides he even admitted the right side. He loved so much to multiply his souls that he had among them one soul at least that was saved. He desired all beautiful things—even God.

His frightful fallacy was that he would not see that there is reason in everything, even in religion and morality. Universality is a contradiction in terms. You cannot be everything if you are anything. If you wish to be white all over, you must austerely resist the temptation to have green spots or yellow stripes. If you wish to be good all over, you must resist the spots of sin or the stripes of servitude. It may be great fun to be many-sided ; but however many sides one has there cannot be one of them which is complete and rounded innocence. A polygon can have an infinite number of sides ; but no one of its sides can be a circle.

JOHN RUSKIN

MEN are constantly saying true things without really thinking them true; there is a great deal of difference between a truth and a true speech, for a true speech implies a true speaker. One of the glib phrases which one hears everywhere, for instance, is this, that we must get some way away from a great man in order to appreciate him. Now there is a truth in this; but have most of us ever found any truth in it? Nothing is worse than the physical metaphors that are used in the matter. A physical metaphor is never an idea, it is only an attempt to help out or re-inforce an idea. When people say that a great man is like a mountain, that we cannot see him when we are under his shadow, but must look back at him from more distant plains, they mean nothing at all. A great man is not in the least like a mountain. There is no kind of really intelligible idea involved in comparing a poet to a peak. We cannot see a mountain when we are close to it because the whole point of a mountain is that it has a physical size unrelated to our physical power of sight, that it cannot get itself into our focus or get itself mirrored on the human mind. But the whole point of a poet is that he can become related to our vision. The whole point of a poet is that he does know how to get himself into the human focus and mirror himself on the human mind. In so far as a mountain is too big to be taken in, it is all the more a mountain. But in so far as a poet is too big to be taken in, he is all the less a poet, for the poet means the man who can express himself; the poet means the man who can make himself understood. That the mountain cannot explain itself until it is dwarfed by distance is a weakness in the mountain. That it is too large to grasp is not a part of the strength of the mountain; it is a part of the huge helplessness of the mountain. The mountain is unimaginable because it is half-witted; rather the mountain is unimaginable because it is dead. It cannot explain itself because it has not intelligence as a man has. The man cannot imagine the mountain, but far less can the mountain imagine him.

I take this current figure as an example of the fallacy of all such cheap physical parallels. None of these things describes why a thinker or artist whose sole and special gift is explaining himself should yet be so strangely unable to explain himself to those nearest to him, to those whom he knows best. None of this explains why a prophet should be without honour in his own country or in his own epoch. A mountain cannot convince those near to it because a mountain cannot contract into a small picture of itself, it cannot reduce itself to scale. But the whole essence of art is that it contracts and reduces itself to scale. Those who talk of the artist nature swelling and expanding, those who talk of the outbreak, licence and overflowing of art are people with no sort of feeling of what art is. Art means diminution. If what you want is largeness, the universe as it is is large enough for anybody. Art exists solely in order to create a miniature universe, a working model of the universe, a toy universe which we can play with as a child plays with a toy theatre.

Yet with all this the fact remains that great men, especially such great men as Ruskin and the more combative critics of the nineteenth century, will require separation and distance before we can appreciate them justly. The real reason of this lies, I think, in something quite different from the average imagery about mere bulk. The reason most probably is one which can be more correctly stated by saying that such combative figures produce a reaction which is almost simultaneous with their energy. Yet this again is a metaphor drawn from physical science and is therefore futile. The most approximately exact statement would perhaps be this : that any man who speaks truth and speaks anything less than the full and divine truth draws attention to all the doctrines that he himself omits. Men grow angrier with him for the two or three things which he states wrongly than for the two or three hundred that he states rightly ; his incompleteness exasperates exactly because he is plausibly and apparently complete. This is the case with all the nineteenth-century prophets, and especially the case with Ruskin. He has very specially the disadvantage of being nearly right, therefore of exasperating us by being wrong. We do not disagree with Ruskin as we disagree with the great decisive philosophers who are our decisive opponents or offer to us decisive alternatives. We do not disagree with Ruskin as we might disagree with Lucretius or with Calvin or with Mahomet or with Professor Haeckel. We disagree with Ruskin as we disagree with a friend gone wrong ; with a man who ought to understand and does not ; or (in some cases I think) who does understand but will not. For the irritation against an enemy is a sudden and exceptional passion ; but the irritation against a friend is a thing that grows and bears fruit like a living orchard. It is possible to be content with our enemies ; it is not possible to be content with our friends. Our irritation against a friend always arises, I think, from the good that he has suggested and has not fulfilled ; and this is exactly the feeling which a modern man has about Ruskin.

Partly the reaction against Ruskin has been due to a consciousness in the man himself that he was restless and partisan. He was irritating because he was irritated. It was said that Carlyle wrote twenty volumes in praise of silence ; it would be fairer to say that Ruskin was perpetually restless in advocating rest. All this should be said and has here been said as an essential preliminary; because this reaction against the nineteenth-century prophet is coming, and indeed has come. There will be a reaction against Ruskin as there was against Dr. Johnson. And there will be a return of Ruskin as there has been a return of Dr. Johnson.

I do not mean merely that there will be a return to the appreciation of his art and style, because there could not possibly be any reaction against that. If there were an age which did not realize that Ruskin wrote great English, it would be an age that had ceased to write English at all; probably an imperial age. Nor is his purely technical triumph wholly unconnected with his philosophy. The main thing that Ruskin existed to preach was this: that life (in the vital sense of vitality) is not a thing of gasps and spasms, but a thing consecutive, interdependent, nay laborious. Life that is alive, he meant, is continuous. Life that is alive is even conventional. The hailstones fall in reckless and scattered independence because the hailstones are dead. The Virginia creeper falls in one connected chain, because the Virginia creeper is alive. Dull savages advance into battle individually and at random; great civilized armies like those of Napoleon or the Crusades advance in long lines of coherence and necessity. But that is only because the lawless fighters are more dead; the ordered fighters are more alive. Now in this respect Ruskin can claim that highest element of greatness, the fact that the meaning and the style are identical. We in the modern very ignorant world have to use short and explosive sentences, like the volleys of the dead hailstones. But Ruskin's long rolling sentences, with their triumphant rise and fall, were themselves expressions of his belief in continuity, and the sublime curves of history. A Ruskin sentence is long as the swinging creeper is long; it is long as the line of the Napoleonic army was long. It is long because it is continuous and because it is alive.

Like all the fighters of his time, Ruskin is under one great disadvantage; that of victory. He has convinced the old, heavy and half-witted utilitarian world; his main historical theories are commonplaces among educated men. Some may or may not think the Middle Ages a nice civilization, but we all know that it was a civilization. The idea that Medievalism was barbaric is now relegated to quite obscure and uninstructed corners—for instance, to the daily papers. A man may be bored with Amiens Cathedral, but he does not now say that he is bored with its extreme savagery and superstition. He says, as has always been said by the man bored with Dante, that he is bored with its extreme civilization. So far no one now quarrels with what Ruskin said, the only quarrel can be with how he said it.

There is a truth in the statement that Ruskin was egotistical. But the truth in the statement is not such as is supposed by most of those who make it. The great majority of casual critics call Ruskin egotistical when they mean that he is dogmatic. As far as that goes there is no evidence at all of his egotism. To be dogmatic and to be egotistic are not only not the same thing, they are opposite things. Suppose, for instance, that a vague sceptic eventually joins the Catholic Church. In that act he has at the same moment become less egotistic and become more dogmatic. The dogmatist is by the nature of the case not egotistical, because he believes that there is some solid obvious and objective truth outside him which he has perceived and which he invites all men to perceive. And the egotist is in the majority of cases not dogmatic, because he has no need to isolate one of his notions as being related to truth; all his notions are equally interesting because they are related to him. The true egotist is as much interested in his own errors as in his own truth; the dogmatist is interested only in the truth, and only in the truth because it is true. At the most the dogmatist believes that he is in the truth; but the egotist believes that the truth, if there is such a thing, is in him.

In so far as Ruskin was dogmatic he was divine. In so far as he was saying that he was right and that all the other people were wrong he was doing what every healthy man ought to do, nay, he was more than healthy; he was humble. There are not many generalizations that can be made about the relations between the morals and the manners of men. Cleanliness may be next to godliness as the proverb says, or godliness may be next to cleanliness and a bad second, as the modern aristocracy says; but the fact certainly remains that some of the best men the world has ever seen have been dirty, and that some of the worst men that will ever go to hell are clean. There are not many statements that a man can make about the things that a man does in connection with the thing that he is. But this generalization is almost always safe: that a man who talks like a torrent for hours on end is a humble man. Dr. Johnson was dogmatic and humble; Mr. Bernard Shaw was dogmatic and humble. The proud man will scarcely ever lay down the law. The proud man will scarcely ever talk too much. He will lie in wait and drop in the epigram where it is exactly needed. He will feast upon speechless superiority, while the modest and unconscious man goes on like Niagara explaining the principles of socialism or the humours of his eldest son. The humble man will be always talkative; for he is interested in his subject and knows that it is best shown in talk. But the proud man will be generally silent; for he is not interested in his subject but in himself. And he knows that he looks best when he is not talking.

First of all therefore let us clear Ruskin of egotism on all such counts as these; let us clear him of egotism in so far that he was long, loquacious, emphatic, explanatory, taking his subject seriously, bothering and blustering at the reader. In all this he was merely simple and sincere. In so far as he was a bully he was an essentially modest man. It is true that he applied dogmatism to things to which dogmatism cannot be applied. It is true that the things about which he was serious were very often exactly the things about which man ought not to be serious—taste, ornament, art, criticism. It is true even that in him with all his Puritanism had been effected something of that inversion which marks the aesthete; I mean the taking of light things too seriously and of serious things too lightly. It was partly because he did make too much of understanding a light subject like art that he could not (apparently) understand at all an important subject like liberty. But when all this is conceded it remains true that his outpourings of passionate assertion on the subject of art were the outpourings of a simple and sincere spirit; the outpourings of a modest heart and not of an egotistic one. Not upon this ground, if upon any, will we accuse him of egotism. Nevertheless there was mingling with all his honesty a certain curious kind of egotism, and in order to explain its nature it is necessary to look back for a moment at a phrase employed above: at the passage in which I said that the true egotist was as much interested in his own errors as in his own truth. This is the real test of whether man has only a righteous trust in his own divine intellect, or whether he has also a morbid pleasure in the mere contemplation of his own human ego. The entirely honest man will have no doubt that he is right: and he will wish to assert it; but he will also have no doubt that he was wrong: and he will wish to forget it. He will grasp his truth like gold. But he will drop his errors like hot bricks. But if there be in him any trace or version of that disease which Meredith satirized in Sir Willoughly Patterne, then he will treasure up his errors and fondle them and turn them over, and perhaps love them more than his truths. This, wherever it occurs, is really a mark of egotism. And this did really occur in the case of Ruskin.

It is a good sign of health in a writer if he thinks a book irrevocable. If the writer is very healthy he will probably regard the book as an irrevocable mistake. But in any case there is something so sacred and final about the giving forth of anything organic that most people with sound instincts will always regard it as something like the birth of a child: a child who may grow up well or ill. Like the birth of a child it is the giving of liberty to something. Henceforth the thing we have made is truly sundered from us, as we are sundered from God. In some atmospheres, however, there has arisen a very bad artistic habit of going over and over artistic work and talking about it as if no one could ever get tired of the subject. Mr. George Moore has specially distinguished himself by purring over his work and petting it as a cat does a mouse, gently commending this and gently lamenting that, as if it were the character of some erring but adorable friend. This fashion is bad everywhere; and into this fashion Ruskin fell. It is this habit in him and this alone, I think, that really irritates us in his later works. I can read a page of his dogmatism with pleasure. But I cannot endure the little notes that he puts at the bottom of the page to point out where he made a mistake and how much he has grown since he made it. That is real vanity; that is real self-love. He is not an egotist when he says that he is right. But he is an egotist when he says that he was wrong.

Such mere iteration of his own individuality (as distinct from his own convictions) was a weakness that grew on him mainly in his later years. It was probably the result of that self-realization in a particular dramatic part which is the nemesis of so many picturesque and partisan writers. It is a good thing to tell a half-truth so long as one thinks that it is the whole truth. But when an enthusiast discovers through experience and sympathy that there is another half of the truth that he has not told, then there is presented to him a perilous alternative. He can go on to the whole truth. In that case he will become more wise, but he will look more ordinary; his special colour, mixed with the complementary colours, will turn into the white light of common day. Perhaps that was what happened to Shakespeare when he went down to buy a farm in Warwickshire. On the one hand, then, he may accept the whole truth; on the other hand he may exaggerate his half-truth, knowing it to be a half-truth. This is what Ruskin did. He could not abandon the youthful pleasures of fanaticism; he refused to grow mellow with age. And young fanaticism cultivated in old age, like young love cultivated in old age, turned sour and unwholesome. It made his work pointed and energetic to the last. But there was something fretful and insecure about it because he was being consciously and deliberately one-sided. In this one cannot but feel that he falls a little below, not only the great men who ended simply and serenely like Shakespeare or Browning, but even below men who were immensely his inferiors in real intellectual courage and vision—men, for instance, like Herbert Spencer. Herbert Spencer lived in a very small mental world, but it was a complete one. He was bounded in a nutshell, but counted himself a king of infinite space. He thought he was telling the whole truth like a medieval philosopher, like a medieval philosopher he would have nothing less than the whole truth. To the medieval thinker the man "with a message" was simply a heretic, that is a nuisance because he only told part of the truth. Herbert Spencer was very like a smaller Thomas Aquinas ; he was the last of the medievals. Herbert Spencer, who thought all Gothic ornament barbarous, was nevertheless much more medieval than John Ruskin, who celebrated every crumbling cloister and every splintered spire.

W. E. HENLEY: POET

THE changes that pass over great societies are often too big to be seen. That is they are too big to be summarized under a public name; but it is a gross mistake to suppose that each of them is not felt as a private fact. Every man feels the faith or the sin; but every man feels it as something peculiar to himself. It is the most secret part of every separate man that makes up a real social movement. The general philosophy is drawn not from what everybody says, but rather from what everybody does not say, but feels the more. Public opinion is made up of all the most peculiarly private opinions. Hence we always find a paradox in the fashion of speech and thought. The changes which men in any age are always talking about are never the changes that are really going on. The changes that are really going on are not those which men pompously applaud when they get together, but those which they vigorously promote when they get by themselves. For instance, England was turned from an agricultural to a commercial country, while people were talking publicly about things quite different; chiefly about whether Charles I's head ought to have been cut off. But because the change came privately, do not suppose that it came unconsciously. On the contrary, it was quite specially conscious because it was quite specially private. Every man was publicly interested in Charles I's head; but every man was privately interested in making money at any cost. And the mad factory chimneys we see everywhere, and the monstrous cities in which we walk, have been created, not by public speeches, but by private thoughts.

Now in the whole literature in the later nineteenth century there was an analogous process; a process which every man felt inside himself and which was yet not much mentioned in the many open debates about art. The change I think was this: that every literary man began consciously to consider himself as a character in a play. He exaggerated his own oddities because he had to conflict with other and opposite oddities. He was the black spot in the picture; someone else was the white. In all the most striking writers of our own time one can feel this picturesque and partisan quality, this quality which assumes the existence of dialogue and of different figures. One can feel it for instance in Mr. Rudyard Kipling and Mr. Bernard Shaw; one can feel the footlights at their feet. Nothing could be more different from this than the old, especially the medieval conception of the function of a man. The medievals believed that one man should have in his head the balance of the whole Universe; a smaller cosmos, but still a cosmos. The medievals thought that a man should have inside his skull a little sun and a little moon, and yet littler stars, all drawn justly and to scale. Every man should have the equipoise of everything. There must be no conscious pitting of red against green according to the medievals; every man as far as his intellect went must be perfect even as his Father in heaven was perfect. The last of the medievals in England was Herbert Spencer.

This modern literary method, that of exaggerating one's own peculiarities as if one were playing in a farce, gave the world a number of arresting and exciting personalities. Its great defect however was this: that it tended to give many men quite false personalities. I mean that even great men sometimes took so totally wrong a view of themselves that much of their work was wasted. They preferred their own masks to their own faces. They painted themselves so fiercely for the footlights that they concealed their own original good looks. It is only these men who had real reputations to spoil and spoilt them who are of any interest in literary history. We need not concern ourselves with mere imbeciles and impostors. We are not troubled about asses in a lion's skin. The only interesting cases are just those two or three cases of one lion dressing up in the skin of another.

One of these curious cases is that of W. E. Henley. He was a man who really suffered from the histrionic habit. He was a man of large heart who deliberately narrowed his heart. He was a man of large brain who deliberately narrowed his brain. He was a man thoroughly by nature a poet who forced himself, against all his own emotional trend, to be a boisterous and topical balladmonger. The critics of the future will have to take a great deal of trouble to extricate the real Henley from under the heavy accretions of the fictitious or dramatic Henley. But they will take the trouble; for they will be digging up gold.

No critic will ever be accused of misrepresenting Henley; the only man who misrepresented Henley was Henley himself. If we read those poems in which Henley was striking a deep note, as distinct from those in which he was thumping a tin kettle, we shall not find it at all difficult without having ever known him, to say what kind of man he was. He was a sad, sensitive and tender-hearted pessimist, who endured pain that came from nowhere, and enjoyed pleasure that came from nowhere, with the exquisite appreciation of some timid child in Maeterlinck's plays. He was not so much a Stoic as a tragic Epicurean. But he had this truly sublime quality in the highest type of Epicurean; that he enjoyed a pleasure so much that it reconciled him even to pain. He certainly believed (in his soul) that the rule of the universe was bad. But his glory was that he was ready to accept the rule for the sake of the exceptions. He enjoyed a red rose so poignantly and perfectly that he was ready to go through thorns for it, even though it was only an accident of the tree and not its crown. His poetry rose to its noblest height when he spoke of the strange joy of having snatched some good from an evil world. This led him to dwell much upon the past; and to him memory was a kind of intoxication. Neither he nor anyone else ever wrote anything much better or more real in its own way than those lines about things already secured.

> What is to come we know not. But we know
> That what has been was good—was good to show,
> Better to hide, and best of all to bear.
> We are the masters of the days that were:
> We have lived, we have loved, we have suffered
> even so.
> Shall we not take the ebb, who had the flow?
> Life was our friend. Now, if it be our foe—
> Dear, though it spoil and break us!—need we care
> What is to come?

That is the true Henley; and as I have said it is not very difficult to understand him. He was what every poet must be who shares the unbelief of his age; a man melancholy though not without happiness; a man reconciled to a second best. A poet who has lost his gods must always be like a lover who has lost his love and has married a sensible woman. For the earth which Henley enjoyed has never been the original starting point of men's thoughts or labours. Heaven was man's first love; and the earth is only a substitute; even when it is not only a marriage of convenience.

Unfortunately in his life-time, and especially in his later years, Henley hid himself behind the mask of what he thought he ought to stand for. Somebody told him, or he somehow got into his head that he was the representative of rude energy and militant empire. His talents were entirely in the other direction. So far from specializing in strength he describes in his most penetrating poems a condition of beautiful weakness. So far from being by nature a prophet of the British Empire he had not the temperament to be a prophet of his own town or street. He did not believe in them enough; he did not believe much in anything. There were some things (it is true) which he definitely disbelieved in; he certainly had a sincere hatred for democracy and for Christian morals. But positive belief involves a certain simple fixity of the intellect which was not at all a part of his personality. He did not really believe even in the stone of the street or the stars in the sky. But he had this strange quality of a great imagination about him; that he could enjoy things even without believing in them.

This quite false conception of himself as a Raw Head and Bloody Bones produced a crop of poems which are not in Henley's good manner or even in his bad manner; they are not in Henley's manner at all. It would be untrue to say that Henley was ever a hypocrite; but some of his poems are hypocritical. "The Song of the Sword" is, I am afraid, hypocritical. It is all about the Lord and the Sword; two things that Henley knew nothing whatever about. Of the sword he had no grasp or experience, and in the Lord he didn't believe. The heavy Old Testament manner of the whole thing was utterly alien to his true nature which was sensitive and modern, exquisitely attuned to pleasure and to pain. He was not a solemn youth like David; he was an Epicurean invalid. A man more unmilitary cannot be conceived; if he had ever held a sword in his hand, he would have been filled either with pain at having to inflict wounds or with pleasure in inflicting them. Both these emotions are feminine and unsoldierly. And the most painful evidence of all of his unfitness for such topics can be found in this; that when he was attempting to be specially masculine he always came near to that most unmasculine of all ideas—cruelty.

But it is not with the false Henley, but the true Henley that the world will deal. He caused his own exquisite voice to be drowned in the clamour of his own quite fictitious reputation as a sort of a political ruffian. He drowned his own voice with his own drum. But anyone who cares to-day to take up one of his books of poems will suddenly find himself in an atmosphere utterly unexpected and very calm. He will break into a sudden stillness. He will read a few quiet poems about grey streets and silver sunsets. He will find that the poet has a peculiar power of describing the voiceless and neglected corners of a great city; the little grass-grown squares, the little streets that lead nowhere. The poet feels the lost parts of London as more lost than the lost parts of the wilderness; and he loves them more. He has an almost eerie power of realizing certain aimless emotions of an empty afternoon. All will seem full of a kind of quiet irrelevance; and yet the very foundations of the reader's heart will be moved. The sadness will only seem an expression of the sacred value of things; and as he walks home at evening after reading such a book, every paving-stone and lamp-post will be pathetic because it is precious. Nay, the world will seem brittle because it is precious; as if it might be broken, by accident.

LOUISA ALCOTT

IT IS very good for a man to talk about what he does not understand; as long as he understands that he does not understand it. Agnosticism (which has, I am sorry to say, almost entirely disappeared from the modern world) is always an admirable thing, so long as it admits that the thing which it does not understand may be much superior to the mind which does not understand it. Thus if you say that the cosmos is incomprehensible, and really mean (as most moderns do) that it is not worth comprehending; then it would be much better for your Greek agnosticism if it were called by its Latin name of ignorance. But there is one thing that any man can fairly consider incomprehensible, and yet in some ways superior. There is one thing that any man may worry about, and still respect; I mean any woman. The deadly and divine cleavage between the sexes has compelled every woman and every man, age after age, to believe without understanding; to have faith without any knowledge.

Upon the same principle it is a good thing for any man to have to review a book which he cannot review. It is a good thing for his agnosticism and his humility to consider a book which may be much better than he can ever understand. It is good for a man who has seen many books which he could not review because they were so silly, to review one book which he cannot review because it is so wise. For wisdom, first and last, is the characteristic of women. They are often silly, they are always wise. Commonsense is uncommon among men; but commonsense is really and literally a common sense among women. And the sagacity of women, like the sagacity of saints, or that of donkeys, is something outside all questions of ordinary cleverness and ambition. The whole truth of the matter was revealed to Mr. Rudyard Kipling when the spirit of truth suddenly descended on him and he said: "Any woman can manage a clever man; but it requires a rather clever woman to manage a fool."

The wisdom of women is different; and this alone makes the review of such books by a man difficult. But the case is stronger. I for one will willingly confess that the only thing on earth I am frightfully afraid of is a little girl. Female children, she babies, girls up to the age of five are perfectly reasonable; but then all babies are reasonable. Grown girls and women give us at least glimpses of their meaning. But the whole of the period between a girl who is six years old and a girl who is sixteen is to me an abyss not only of mystery, but of terror. If the Prussians were invading England, and I were holding a solitary outpost, the best thing they could do would be to send a long rank or regiment of Prussian girls of twelve, from which I should fly, screaming.

Now the famous books of Miss Alcott are all about little girls. Therefore, my first impulse was to fly screaming. But I resisted this impulse, and I read the books; and I discovered, to my immeasurable astonishment, that they were extremely good. *Little Women* was written by a woman for women—for little women. Consequently it anticipated realism by twenty or thirty years; just as Jane Austen anticipated it by at least a hundred years. For women are the only realists; their whole object in life is to pit their realism against the extravagant, excessive, and occasionally drunken idealism of men. I do not hesitate. I am not ashamed to name Miss Alcott and Miss Austen. There is, indeed, a vast division in the matter of literature (an unimportant matter), but there is the same silent and unexplained assumption of the feminine point of view. There is no pretence, as most unfortunately occurred in the case of another woman of genius, George Eliot, that the writer is anything else but a woman, writing to amuse other women, with her awful womanly irony. Jane Austen did not call herself George Austen; nor Louisa Alcott call herself George Alcott. These women refrained from that abject submission to the male sex which we have since been distressed to see; the weak demand for masculine names and for a part in merely masculine frivolities; parliaments, for instance. These were strong women; they classed parliament with the public-house. But for another and better reason, I do not hesitate to name Miss Alcott by the side of Jane Austen; because her talent, though doubtless inferior, was of exactly the same kind. There is an unmistakable material truth about the thing; if that material truth were not the chief female characteristic, we should most of us find our houses burnt down when we went back to them. To take but one instance out of many, and an instance that a man can understand, because a man was involved, the account of the quite sudden and quite blundering proposal, acceptance, and engagement between Jo and the German professor under the umbrella, with parcels falling off them, so to speak, every minute, is one of the really human things in human literature; when you read it you feel sure that human beings have experienced it often; you almost feel that you have experienced it yourself. There is something true to all our own private diaries in the fact that our happiest moments have happened in the rain, or under some absurd impediment of absurd luggage. The same is true of a hundred other elements in the story. The whole affair of the children acting the different parts in *Pickwick*, forming a childish club under strict restrictions, in order to do so; all that is really life, even where it is not literature. And as a final touch of human truth, nothing could be better than the way in which Miss Alcott suggests the borders and the sensitive privacy of such an experiment. All the little girls have become interested, as they would in real life, in the lonely little boy next door; but when one of them introduces him into their private club in imitation of *Pickwick*, there is a general stir of resistance; these family fictions do not endure being considered from the outside.

All that is profoundly true; and something more than that is profoundly true. For just as the boy was an intruder in that club of girls, so any masculine reader is really an intruder among this pile of books. There runs through the whole series a certain moral philosophy, which a man can never really get the hang of. For instance, the girls are always doing something, pleasant or unpleasant. In fact, when they have not to do something unpleasant, they deliberately do something else. A great part, perhaps the more godlike part, of a boy's life, is passed in doing nothing at all. Real selfishness, which is the simplest thing in the world to a boy or man, is practically left out of the calculation. The girls may conceivably oppress and torture each other; but they will not indulge or even enjoy themselves—not, at least, as men understand indulgence or enjoyment. The strangest things are taken for granted; as that it is wrong in itself to drink champagne. But two things are quite certain; first, that even from a masculine standpoint, the books are very good; and second, that from a feminine standpoint they are so good that their admirers have really lost sight even of their goodness. I have never known, or hardly ever known, a really admirable woman who did not confess to having read these books. Haughty ladies confessed (under torture) that they liked them still. Stately Suffragettes rose rustling from the sofa and dropped *Little Women* on the floor, covering them with public shame. At learned ladies' colleges, it is, I firmly believe, handed about secretly, like a dangerous drug. I cannot understand this strange and simple world, in which unselfishness is natural, in which spite is easier than self-indulgence. I am the male intruder, like poor Mr. Laurence and I withdraw. I back out hastily, bowing. But I am sure that I leave a very interesting world behind me.

SHERLOCK HOLMES

I

THE RETURN of Sherlock Holmes to the *Strand Magazine* some years after his death, put a finishing touch to the almost heroic popularity of a figure whose reality was like the universally admitted reality of some old hero of medieval fable. Just as Arthur and Barbarossa were to return again, men felt that this preposterous detective must return again. He had emerged out of the unreality of literature into the glowing reality of legend, and in proof of this he has inherited the most widespread and pathetic of the characteristics of legendary heroes; that characteristic which makes men incredulous of their death. A slight and fantastic figure in a fugitive and ironical type of romance, he may seem too insignificant a subject for such a description. Nevertheless the fact remains that Mr. Conan Doyle's hero is probably the only literary creation since the creations of Dickens which has really passed into the life and language of the people, and become a being like John Bull or Father Christmas. It is remarkable to notice that although we possess many writers whose popularity is attested by enormous sales and general discussion, there is hardly one of them except Conan Doyle in this instance whose characters are familiar to everyone as types and symbols, as Pecksniff was the type of hypocrisy or Bumble of officialism. Rudyard Kipling, for example, is undoubtedly a popular writer. But if we were to go up to any man in the street and say that a particular problem would have puzzled Strickland he would receive it with a very different expression of countenance to that which he would wear if we said that it would puzzle Sherlock Holmes. Mr. Kipling's stories give inexhaustible intellectual delight, but the personality which we remember is the personality of the story, not the personality of the character. We remember the action, but forget the actors. In no other current creation except Sherlock Holmes does the character succeed, so to speak, in breaking out of the book as a chicken breaks out of the egg. The characters of Dickens had this capacity. The *Pickwick Papers* only prepared Sam Weller for us; after the book was written, Sam Weller is greater than the book. We can apply his philosophy for ourselves; we can continue his adventures in our dreams.

The fact that Sherlock Holmes alone has succeeded in familiarising himself at once with the cultured and the uncultured and turned his name into almost as descriptive a word as Dr. Guillotin or Captain Boycott, involves certain conclusions, which are for the most part worthy and reassuring. The phenomenon corrects finally, for example, much of the foolish and foppish talk about the public preferring books because they are bad. The stories of Sherlock Holmes are very good stories; they are perfectly graceful and conscientious works of art. The thread of irony which runs through all the solemn impossibilities of the narrative gives it the position of a really brilliant addition to the great literature of nonsense. The notion of the greatness of an intellect, proved by its occupation with small things instead of with great, is an original departure; it constitutes a kind of wild poetry of the commonplace. The intellectual clues and cruces upon which the development of each story turns are perhaps incredible as fact, but they are thoroughly solid and important as logic; they are such problems as a great lawyer might extract from two bottles of champagne;

they are full of the very revelry of reason. The figure of Conan Doyle's detective is, in its own wild and trifling way, good literature.

Now, there are in London more than nine hundred and ninety-nine detective stories and fictitious detectives, nearly all of which are bad literature, or rather not literature at all. If, as the saying goes, the public likes books because they are bad, it would not be the fact that the one fictitious detective who is familiar to the whole public is the one fictitious detective who is a work of art. The fact of the matter is that ordinary men prefer certain kinds of work, good or bad, to certain other kinds of work, good or bad, which they have a perfect and obvious right to do. They prefer romance, farce, and everything that concerns the material diplomacy of life, to psychological delicacies or the more secret humours of existence. But, preferring a certain thing, they prefer it good if they can get it. The man in the street may prefer ale to crême de menthe, but it is nonsense to say that he prefers bad ale to good ale. He does not read George Meredith because he does not want that kind of book, however good it is, and he would not want it however bad it was. Surely we all know that there are hundreds of pigmy Merediths eternally engaged upon their unsightly embroideries and their bungling dissections. Bad literature is not confined to romance. The whole army of men in the street is scarcely so large as the army of young gentlemen who make it their business to despise the man in the street. Yet the sonnets of these young symbolists and the novels of these young psychologists are not sold like hot cakes upon bookstalls or read aloud in uproarious inn-parlours. The man who writes such literature as *The Egoist* has no right to expect to be as popular as Conan Doyle any more than a man who made incomparable astronomical telescopes would expect them to sell like umbrellas. But it would be odd to deduce from this that the ordinary man has a weird and occult tenderness for a bad umbrella.

II

All English people have read the stories about Sherlock Holmes. Work like this is so good of its kind that it is difficult to endure patiently the talk of people who are occupied only in pointing out that it is not work of some other kind. The specific quality of a story of this sort is strictly what may be called wit; it is obliged to have some definite invention, construction and point, like a joke in the comic papers. Such work is inexpressibly superior to most mediocre serious work. There has to be something in it; it cannot be an entire imposture. A man can pretend to be wise; a man cannot pretend to be witty. His jokes may be much worse in your opinion than they are in his opinion; but after all they must be jokes; they cannot be entirely shapeless mysteries, like many modern works of philosophy.

Many men can make an epic who could not make an epigram. What is true of the comic anecdote is true also of that extended anecdote, the sensational story with a point to it. All real philosophy is apocalyptic, and if a man can give us revelations of heaven it is certainly better than giving us horrible revelations of high life. But I would rather have the man who devotes a short story to saying that he can solve the problem of a murder in Margate than the man who devotes a whole book to saying that he cannot solve the problem of things in general.

Sir Arthur Conan Doyle certainly weakened his excellent series of stories by being occasionally serious; especially he weakened it by introducing a sort of sneer at Edgar Allan Poe's Dupin, with whom he sustained no comparison. Sherlock Holmes's bright notions were like bright Cockney flowers grown in very shallow soil in a suburban garden; Dupin's were flowers growing on a vast, dark tree of thought. Hence Dupin, when he quits the subject of crime, talks in the tongue of permanent culture of the relations of imagination to analysis or of the relations of the supernatural to law. But the greatest error of the Sherlock Holmes conception remains to to be remarked: I mean the error which represented the detective as indifferent to philosophy and poetry, and which seemed to imply that philosophy and poetry would not be good for a detective. Here he is at once eclipsed by the bolder and more brilliant brain of Poe, who carefully states that Dupin not only admired and trusted poetry, but was himself a poet. Sherlock Holmes would have been a better detective if he had been a philosopher, if he had been a poet, nay, if he had been a lover. It is remarkable to notice (I assume that you are as intimate with Dr. Watson's narratives as you should be)—it is remarkable to notice that the very same story in which the biographer describes Holmes's inaccessibility to love and such emotions, and how necessary it was to the clear balance of his logic, is the very same story in which Holmes is beaten by a woman because he does not know whether a certain man is her fiancé or her lawyer. If he had been in love he might have known well enough.

The only real danger is that Conan Doyle, by spreading the notion that practical logic must be unpoetical, may have encouraged the notion, too common already, that imagination must be absent-minded. It is a false and dangerous doctrine that the poet must be absent-minded. The purely imaginative man could never be absent-minded. He would perceive the significance of things near to him as clearly as he perceived the significance of things far off. In the highest imaginative sense man has no right whatever to forget his tea-cup because he is thinking about Plato. If he does not understand his tea-cup which he has seen, how shall he understand Plato whom he has not seen? The best and last word of mysticism is an almost agonising sense of the preciousness of everything, the preciousness of the whole universe, which is like an exquisite and fragile vase, and among other things the preciousness of other people's tea-cups. The last and best word of mysticism is not lavishness, but rather a sublime and sacred economy.

The perfect mystic would be always socially alert. The perfect mystic would be always correctly dressed. To such heights of transcendentalism some of us may find it difficult to soar; and such honest and unselfconscious failure, though it is certainly a weakness, is not an unpardonable or inhuman one. Some of the best men in the world—Dr. Johnson, for instance—have been specially remarkable for being conventional in theory and unconventional in practice. But if once a man is unconventional in theory, then the situation is atrocious. It almost certainly means either that a man has no morals or that he has no brains. The type of man does exist who says clearly and deliberately that he does not want to observe the little laws that surround him, that he is proud of being absent-minded, that he is proud of his disdain of detail. Whenever this occurs it certainly arises in another and most literal sense from absence—of Mind.

The real moral of the popularity of the adventures of Sherlock Holmes lies in the existence of a great artistic neglect. There are a large number of perfectly legitimate forms of art which are almost entirely neglected by good artists—the detective story, the farce, the book of boyish adventure, the melodrama, the music-hall song. The real curse of these things is not that they are too much regarded, but that they are not regarded enough; that they are despised even by those who write them. Conan Doyle triumphed and triumphed deservedly, because he took his art seriously, because he lavished a hundred little touches of real knowledge and genuine picturesqueness on the police novelette. He substituted for the customary keen eyes and turned-up collar of the conventional detective a number of traits, external and pictorial, indeed, but honestly appropriate to the logical genius, traits such as an immeasurable love of music and an egotism which was abstract and, therefore, almost unselfish. Above all, he surrounded his detective with a genuine atmosphere of the poetry of London. He called up before the imagination a new and visionary city in which every cellar and alley hid as many weapons as the rocks and heather-bushes of Roderick Dhu. By this artistic seriousness he raised one at least of the popular forms of art to the level which it ought to occupy.

He wrote the best work in a popular form, and he found that because it was the best it was also the most popular. Men needed stories, and had been content to take bad ones; and they were right, for a story in itself is a marvellous and excellent thing, and a bad story is better than no story, just as half a loaf is better than no bread. But when a detective story was written by a man who refused to despise his art, who carried all their dreams to fulfilment, they preferred him to the bungling and irresponsible authors who had catered for them before. It is no discredit to them that psychologies and philosophies had not sated their need for the rush of a climax and the fascination of a riddle. It would be as reasonable to blame men for not accepting cats as watch-dogs, or using pocket-knives as fire-irons. Men must have detective stories; they must have farces and melodramas and comic songs. For anyone who is honest enough to take trouble and invoke inspiration over these other forms, the road lies open to rich and many-coloured fields of undiscovered art.

VICTORIAN BIOGRAPHY AND ALICE MEYNELL

THE Victorian Age suffered from being, not the time in which the domestic spirit was at its highest, but the time when it was at its lowest. It was an age of doubt rather than of doctrine ; and that was precisely the reason why, in most cases, the convictions only remained as conventions. The Victorian domestic biography, of the type of the official biography of Tennyson, failed, not by being domestic, but by being official. The writer did not present the hero as seen from the inside ; but was careful to go a long way off and look at him from the outside, as if he were a public building. The duty of building the sepulchre often meant merely the duty of making it a whited sepulchre. But there is nothing to whitewash about Alice Meynell ; and in her family there has been a tradition older than the Victorian Age and indifferent to all the ages. Hence the book, written by her daughter in a really easy and humorous style, is full of the comments of real children on a real mother.

In the case of Alice Meynell, we may employ a paradox of the mind which doctors sometimes use of the body when they say that a delicate person can be healthy, while a strong person can be diseased. She was healthy and delicate ; but her social surroundings, her critics and even her admirers, tended to talk too much about the delicacy and too little about the health. What always strikes me about her writings is not their fastidiousness but their freshness. She was in a sense fastidious about selecting or rejecting words ; but she selected them because they were fresh, or rejected them because they were not fresh enough. Not everybody will feel this; because we have fallen into a rather false association of ideas about freshness of language. It will sound too comic even for a contrast to mention the name of Alice Meynell with the name of O. Henry. I may even claim some largeness of taste in enormously enjoying them both. I think that O. Henry was possibly the best American poet. There is often in his prose a thread of fancy that is really poetical, though entirely farcical. But his style and language are the reverse of fresh. Those arabesques of slang are full of traditions of travesty; parodies of parodies, desperate misquotations of too familiar quotations, the attempt to give a last twist to infinitely twisted things. It is language on its last legs; and there is a sense in which a comic writer like Henry suffers from the excess of culture. Only our prejudice in favour of America as a New Country (whatever that may mean) disguises what is jaded in this journalistic ingenuity. If it were not American, we should call it Byzantine. At the opposite extreme, Alice Meynell stood for the sort of style which uses words in a primitive fashion. When she said, "light", it was the first light; when she said "shadow", it was the first shadow on the light. I think the most characteristic thing she ever wrote was the little lyric called "Rivers Unknown to Song"; by which she meant the rivers most repeatedly recognised in song; the Nile or the Tiber or the Rhine. Hundreds of poets have praised the antiquity of the rivers when they were really praising the antiquity of the valleys. But she felt suddenly the freshness of the waters themselves; as she would have felt the actual shock of cool water. She was the first to point out that the waters themselves were always fresh:

> But these, they are new, they are fresh ; there's no surprise
> Like their's on earth ; O strange for evermore !
> This moment's Tiber, with his shining eyes,
> Never saw Rome before.

It is not without a mystical moral, which she would have specially approved, about her generation and all newer generations, as each discovers for itself the immortal novelty of Rome.

Now a study of her life does reveal the paradox or perplexity ; that she was surrounded by a world which cared too much for subtlety and did not adequately value her very real simplicity. She saw the primal mystery of light and shade ; but her friends were rather too fond of fine shades. They were rather too fond of her own fine shades ; and of encouraging her to nothing else but fine shades ; and the result is rather to exchange mystery for mystification. With all possible intellectual admiration for Coventry Patmore, it is impossible not to be impatient with the very fine, not to say flimsy shade, which he allowed to pass over their friendship. My whole heart goes out in a warmth of sympathy to Francis Thompson when he interrupted one of their literary readings, at some tense and exquisite moment, by exclaiming, " Here's a go ! Mrs. Meynell ! I've lost the Athenaeum cheque." But my whole heart does not go out to him when he writes her about three pages of tortuous and rather sulky self-analysis ; all because she forgot to read some particular manuscript with him on some particular afternoon. These people were too touchy ; they wounded each other, but they also encouraged each other to be wounded. And my sympathies are altogether with Mrs. Meynell, and I will add with Mr. Meynell, when tender hints are even now thrown out that she sometimes failed in the more officious offices of friendship, through a disposition to mind her own business. I think there is much truth in a suggestion that she ought to have been in a bigger and more regular business. She ought to have been more in the public battle and less in the private bickerings. For she was a fighter ; though a fighter with the rapier. It is a very deadly weapon ; and no critics could be more completely dead than those mockers of Mrs. Johnson or Mrs. Dingley whom she transfixed with so slender a blade.

MR. MASEFIELD'S SHORT STORIES

IF A MAN should have the misfortune to die suddenly while wearing a pink shirt, a violet waistcoat, and a neck-tie of electric blue, with (let us say) scarlet spots, it is the general opinion of the intellectual in the modern world that he would not very easily go to heaven. A person struck by a thunderbolt when in art colours, it is generally felt, would stand a considerably better chance. Now on this delicate point of doctrine I have always felt differently. It appears to me that the fault of the man in pink and blue is a fault of arrangement merely. He tries to have too many incompatible things; he tries to have too many of the divine blessings in one divine moment. But in regarding blue as a divine blessing and scarlet as a divine blessing he is surely quite right. Green is a good thing; scarlet is a good thing; violet is a good thing, and his fierce delight in them is a good thing. When he goes above, the angels will only have to rearrange his costume. Perhaps they will have to affix his bow-tie to some part of his back, in the capacity of wings, or arrange the red spots in a kind of circle round his head; but in any case they will approve his love of loud colours in themselves. His neck-tie is not bluer than the walls of sapphire; his spots not more red than the flaming robes of the martyrs. But about the fate of the art colours I am not so clear; I fear they may find a too congenial position in the shadows and vapours of another place.

As I close a book of Mr. Masefield's short stories, the impression that chiefly remains with me is an impression of the splendour of common colours. These queer and cunning tales of the sea have a hundred other merits, but this happens to be the taste left in the mouth. He has a tropical taste in some ways; in some ways almost a negro one. But here we have the strong colours which my imaginary friend so unfortunately mismanaged, managed shrewdly and well. Here we have colours that would captivate a Cockney used so as to captivate an artist. The strong blue and green of the sea, the strong red and gold of the sunset, the fierce colours of fishes, the startling colours of flowers, are all vivid and yet never, thank God, realistic.

The technique of Mr. Masefield's tales in this matter of colour deserves a word to itself; for it is interesting in no small degree. The chief impression which his pictures produce is the sense of his great love of colour. But, while it is a love of colour, it is, so to speak, a love of primary colour. From the beginning to the end of his books you will hardly find, I think you will never find, any of those mongrel colours so dear to the mongrel modern mind. You will not find any of the nameless colours, the colours that have lost their names in unlawful unions. You will not find the evil purple of the decadents, the greys and greens of Whistler, the greys and browns of Zola, the strange yellow and orange that curled round Aubrey Beardsley, the queer and cruel Oriental reds and ivories that glare from the tropic temples of Kipling. Mr. Masefield uses colour as the old epics or the old ballads loved to use it; very simply and very recurrently. His tales remind us of the ballads in which gold is called red gold three times in a page or the wood is called green every time it is mentioned. Pedants used to smile at this custom, but the simple men who heard the ballads and the wise men who have revived them alike knew better; they knew that the red gold and the green woodland thus continually repeated made a kind of pattern of clear colours, like a child's wall-paper, to be the background of a noble and simple tale.

Mr. Masefield's tales are of a more fantastic pattern than these old English or Scotch ballads; for no tales of the green wood can in their nature be so terrible as the tales of the green sea. But however sprawling or eccentric may be the story he has to tell, the details are always picked out in these plain and infantile colours, like the greenness of woodlands or the redness of gold. And in each case, as we read the passage, we can feel how a modern realist or a modern professor of " word-painting " would have done the thing ; we can feel how much more ingenious he would have been and how much less effective. In one of Mr. Masefield's sketches, for instance, a sketch called " Port of Many Ships", the old sailor describes the manner in which the Day of Judgment shall come upon the sea. And he says that every drowned sailor will rise from the sea " with the green weeds on him". That seems to me like Homer or some grand barbaric classic ; so picturesque, so plain-spoken, so scornful of elaboration, so prosaic, so poetic. The adjective comes with the noun, easily to the mind—and yet the adjective is quite enough to make a coloured picture. And then we think of how the " word-painter " would have dealt with it, with his tortured sentences and his insane epithets. We can imagine the sentence : " Quickly come up sailors, all clogged and clumsied in the weeds of greasy green-umber, crawling with salt wet." Or " The sick sea spits out here and again a sea man bundled in the foul salt foliage, coloured like absinthe". It is so in page after page of these bright and direct descriptions, all full of the colours of a shilling paint-box—which were the colours of Eden. " All her buckets were green," says Mr. Masefield of a fantastic ship, " and in every bucket there were big red roses growing." I know that the word-painter would sit down and try and think of some extraordinary adjective for big red roses. Let me ease his mind by suggesting the word " apoplectic ", which, if he applies it somewhere prominently to a big red rose, will immediately make his fortune. But I will not have this sort of thing in the case of good strong legends of the sea. Mr. Masefield's style, in fact, is symbolised accidentally by himself. In a very weird and, to tell the truth, a somewhat bewildering story called "A Deal of Cards", he describes a sort of mystical negress in "a plain gown of scarlet". That plain gown of scarlet is the garb of Mr. Masefield's muse; as plain as it is scarlet, as scarlet as it is plain.

Mr. Masefield has the true spirit of the ancient childhood of the earth. He has the real spirit of the poets, and he has it precisely in that particular in which the poets and the tellers of fairy-tales most seriously and most decisively differ from the realists of our own day. Mr. Masefield tells a story that is in itself strange, or splendid, or even supernatural, but tells it in the common, graphic language of life. The realist tells a story which is commonplace and trivial, but tells it in the vocabulary of a lunatic asylum. The one describes Polyphemus or Leviathan in the terms applicable to turnips and crockery. The other describes a clerk in Camberwell in terms only suitable to the demons in Pandemonium. It is not my business here to attempt to hold any balance of justice between these two methods of literature, or even to say what is chiefly to be said for one or other of them. Probably they are both right, and both express needs of the soul which we must never underrate or forget. Perhaps the old simple fearlessness and plainness in the presence of the prodigious is rightly to be balanced with our mystery and excitement in the presence of the small. Certainly we ought to be more courageous in the presence of Polyphemus. Certainly, I think, we ought to be more awe-struck and terrified in the presence of the clerk. But for the old tale of prodigies plainly told there is always this one small thing to be said—that children will always like it better. And one of the children who like it better is the writer of the present article. Another, I fancy, is Mr. Masefield.

ERIC GILL AND NO NONSENSE

I SHOULD really be rather curious to know what is made of Mr. Eric Gill's vigorous book *Art Nonsense*, for even I, who sympathise with so many of his primary principles, find them almost too primary to be reduced to any secondary terms. He begins so very much at the right end, that is he begins so very much at the beginning, that there is no getting behind him or treating his absolutes as relative to anything else. And the problem would be equally difficult for the sort of critic whom his friends call modern, and his foes call mad, and the sort of critic whom his friends call sane and his foes call Philistine. Mr. Gill does in a quite definite and dogmatic sense treat art as religious art. And he treats it in such stark and startling contrast with most recent associations of religious art, that all the anti-religious art critics will find their useful and familiar insults frozen on their lips. It is no use to say that Mr. Gill wishes to be a moralist rather than an artist; because people can see for themselves that much of his work consists of balance and proportion as abstract as mathematics: and is often expressed in stern and stubborn stone-cutting which may or may not be carving but is certainly not moralising. It will be absurd to say that Mr. Gill is a Christian craftsman because he is an old-fashioned craftsman; when half his work horrifies the old-fashioned public and turns the elder critics to stone like any Gorgon of Epstein. It is absurd to say that Mr. Gill is sentimental and affected by the anecdotal picture; when he is obviously exactly the opposite. The theory of art he propounds, if anything, does not allow art to be anecdotal enough. It will be utterly hopeless to pretend that Mr. Gill continues what may be called the ethical bias of Ruskin ; since it is obvious on the face of it that what Mr. Gill says is almost exactly the opposite of what Ruskin says. For instance, in the Ruskinian thesis of *The Two Paths*, the beginnings of a realistic treatment of the snake and the apple are represented as the roots of all fruitful art, while the mere balanced diagram of an angel in Celtic ornament is treated as a geometrical prison, from which such a barren art will never escape. Mr. Gill is more likely, on the whole, to regard the realistic apple as that trebly forbidden fruit of " photographic " art, at which the birds pecked in the old anecdote ; and to advise the artist, like the angel, to remain in the eternal liberty of his pure mathematical limitations.

Expressed approximately, in popular language, Mr. Gill's thesis is this. The Victorian moralists allowed the artist to exist, on condition that he represented the wonders of creation. Mr. Gill allows him to exist on condition that he expresses the wonder of creation ; but it all turns on the two senses of the word " creation ", almost in the manner of a pun. To put it another way, the artist is not so much to copy the works of God as to copy the work of God, in the sense of the working of God ; or the way in which God works. There will be in his art the same, or some approximation to the same, spirit and tendency of line and motion and balance ; because there is only one creation and no inspiration from outside it. But the work will rather be that of the child of God making his own smaller world than the servant of God copying the details of the larger one. And as even the Divine Creator pours forth his cataracts in a manner proper to water and not to something else, as he carves even his trees in a style properly to be called wood-carving and not stone-carving, as he hollows the rock in one way and the wave in another, so the human creator also is right to recognise the materials in which his meaning is bodied forth; and to express it in his own materials and not in an imitation of the cosmic materials. As Mr. Gill once expressed it in a speech somewhere, " A sculptor has to make a man; but it has to be a stone man. It has to be the sort of man that God would have made, if He had chosen to make him in stone."

So far as that fundamental thesis is concerned, I think Mr. Gill rams his point home with admirable energy. It is a principle which liberates the artist from the trivial tyranny of mere mimicry. It also liberates the moral spirit of man (which happens to be more important) from any mere stunned submission or trance of fatalism; all the worse, if anything, when it is optimistic fatalism. It is consonant with that original and heroic doctrine of Christianity, which distinguishes the son from the slave, and salutes in his free will the highest crest and signal of his divine origin. God created a creature, and indeed many creatures; but here, we insist, he created a creative creature.

It is when Mr. Gill comes to deal directly with the representative test in art, or what some call " photographic art ", that I am not so sure that I agree with him. Perhaps it would be truer to say that I am not so sure that I understand him. Perhaps it would be truest of all to say that I am not so sure that I understand myself; for it seems to me that in these metaphysical things it is too easily assumed that men understand themselves. To begin with, it is unfair to talk about " photographic art " as an equivalent to representative or realistic art. A camera does not copy the details of every weed and nettle with the pious patience of a Pre-Raphaelite; because a camera is not pious or even patient. A camera does not work out thoroughly the whole scheme of a piece of still life, with the craftsmanship and technical honesty of a Dutch painter; because a camera is not a craftsman; and a camera can no more be honest than dishonest. The English Pre-Raphaelite or the Dutch realist may have taken a wrong view of their business; but they took *some* view of their business. And the view that the mind takes of its function must always be different from the "view" which the camera takes of the landscape. That "view" is not a view or a vision or a version of anything; it is simply something that happened outside the realm of mind. It is a brute collision between mechanics and matter; between the blind sun and the brainless stones. No art ever was this, or ever could be; it has all passed through the mind; and the question is whether the mind may make its effects out of real things or no. I imagine that Mr. Gill, with his generous love of liberty, would say that it may; but I do not think he always makes this part of his argument as clear as the rest. It seems to me that there certainly is something, which is not pure rhythm or balance or movement, but which does affect the imagination and the sense of beauty; something that may be rather darkly described as identity. It is a certain recognition and realisation of things, with the associations of those things and those alone. I warmly and willingly agree that an artist may represent these recognisable things under all sorts of severe conventions or curt symbols, according to the style in which he works. If Mr. Gill chooses to carve an escalloped line of curves across a blank stone, I will admit that they make a rhythmic scheme of decoration. But I will not admit that it does not matter, to my imagination or anybody else's, whether they are meant for sea-waves or birds flying or snakes linked together. I say it matters immensely, because you cannot so much as say the words "sea" or "snakes" without waking a thousand thronging echoes in the human soul. And it is exactly this human soul, according to Mr. Gill, into which we must look to find the true creative forces of art. May I suggest, that, as a fact, a joy in the right realisation of real things is one of the things that we find there? Perhaps the solution of the problem lies somewhere here. Mr. Gill says, "Look inside you, for the wonderful plastic powers that God has given you." Ruskin said, "Look outside you, for the wonderful sea and birds that God has made." But is it so absolutely certain that the sea and birds are outside you? Are not the sea and birds you really look at, when you recall them artistically, things already soaked in your own mystical nature, reshaped and simplified by your own instinct for symbol and design; so that being true to that truth is not merely photographic, but something which quacks call psychological, and sensible men call spiritual? I put this rather in the form of a question than a condemnation; for among my doubts about it is a grave doubt about whether Mr. Gill would really disagree at all. The two outstanding things about this book are; first that it is so original that most people will say it is nonsense; and second, that, in the most emphatic sense, there is no nonsense about it. If there is another word that would occur to me in describing it, after the term "virility", it would be the term "commonsense". It is not Eric Gill's fault if he lives in an age of dirty favouritism and perversion, in which we shall have to wait for some time for commonsense to become common. If his forthright style and fundamental convictions bewilder many people of many groups, possibly even including his own, it will not be because there is anything in him of what moderns call the mystic when they mean the mystagogue; but because he belongs to the great company of those who talk too plainly to be understood.

THE SPIRIT OF PLACE

IN THE greatest of patriotic speeches (tragic, like all true patriotism) it is lamented that the beloved city had not known the things that belong to its peace. A similar phrase would define the failure of almost any community.

There are special things which belong to the peace of special places; a place may find its peace in noise. But it must be its own kind of noise; the noise of carts may be appropriate; the noise of perfect music may be discordant. There is still, as in pagan times, a god of every city, since there is a soul of every city; unless the god build the city, their labour is but lost that build it; unless the soul keep the city, the watchman watcheth but in vain. We shall soon—please God—be engaged in some kind of public attempt to purify and recreate the cities of modern Europe.

Before we enter on that task let us get it clearly into our heads that even if they are perfect they must not be uniform. Let us realise that there is a difference in cities as there is a difference in soils. There is one thing that can be done with a place and another thing that cannot be done with it; there is one kind of perfection that can be given to it and another that cannot be given to it. You can make a mountain village a miserable mountain village or a perfect mountain village, but you cannot make it a perfect sea-port town. You can make hill-men happy or unhappy hill-men, but you cannot make them men of the fens; you may drain the fens, but you do not make them any more like the hills. The same principle is even truer of cities, for in the growth of cities there has been more choice and less accident. By all means let us purify

London; let us reform London. Let us, if you will, remake London. But let us remake it as London, not as Paris or as New York.

There could not be a better instance of the special oddity of the London atmosphere than its relations to literature. In one sense, London is a much less literary city than Paris, but in another sense a much more literary city. One distinction must stare every one in the face; literature is much more publicly and powerfully brought home to the mind in the streets of Paris than in the streets of London. In Paris all the great French authors are worthily represented in the great streets and squares, not only by names but by fine statues and monuments. In London the streets and squares are commonly called after the less known part of the names of aristocrats.

Under the French system Grosvenor Square would probably be called Milton Square and have a huge statue of Milton in the middle. But the London method is so confused that if we did have a square called Milton Square it would probably have a statue of Chaucer in the middle. The one standing case in point is a paradox of almost bewildering complexity. The only square which has a statue of Shakespeare is named after the Earls of Leicester, but is chiefly remembered in connection with an oligarch of briefer tenure, called Baron Grant. Between Grant and Leicester, at any rate, Shakespeare is quite forgotten, and his statue is generally regarded as a kind of joke. Hence it arises, as a characteristic of literary London, that nobody ever remembers, even for a moment, the meaning of the names or the association of the spots.

As a matter of fact, of course, the absence of literary names for London streets is very remarkable; a Frenchman must find it incredible that there is no Shakespeare Street, no Milton Street, no Bacon Street, no Byron Street, no Wordsworth

Street, no Dickens Street, no Keats Street—though the last might be considered cacophonous. But I mean that, apart from this, where there really is an English literary name identical with the name of a place we do not think instinctively of the connection. In Paris on the Quai Voltaire one does really think of Voltaire; there is his great sneering statue to remind one in any case. But, moreover, the mere sight of the straight roads and the strong city would recall the intellect and energy of eighteenth-century France. But I wonder how many men catching a train at Addison Road Station have ever thought of the elegance and the irony of Joseph Addison.

Yet, oddly enough, the very fact that London is not in that sense literary, makes it particularly appropriate as a place for literary men. It is all the easier to dream of or create a work of art in the midst of London, because London is not itself, like Paris or Florence or Venice, a work of art. Many English authors have written about Florence, but most of them have written about it in London. Many "great English poets" have admired Venice, but most great English poets were born in London. No one wishes to write a poem when he is inside a poem. No one composes a drama on the stage.

For the purposes of poetic creation there is required rather a certain atmosphere of quiet, unconsciousness and carelessness; exactly that sort of soundless confusion which can be found, for instance, in a forest. For a forest may be defined as a sort of silent anarchy. These qualities of the forest can really be found to a considerable extent in London. London has the unconsciousness of the forest; for London has grown vaguely and without any plan, and is still strangely lacking in a real common public spirit. London has the variety of the forest; for all historical strata can be found there, and an A.B.C. tea-shop may easily be next door to a mansion which remembers the great aristocracy of the Reformation, or a church which recalls the more democratic atmosphere of the thirteenth century.

It may seem strange to add that London has even the quiet of the forest. There is a certain amount of noise in London, but it might be called dead silence compared with the particular clatter and clamour which belongs to the streets of Paris, and which is the positive product of that splendid impatience which is the deepest fact about the French. It has been well for Europe that the French have been impatient. All the rest of us are only too patient; and but for them should be still asleep under every cowardice and political corruption. But the fact remains that the permanent French capacity for revolution (that is, for intolerance) expresses itself in the very pace of French horses, in the very gestures of French coachmen. If the cracks of their whips come like pistol shots, it is because they would let off pistol shots almost as readily; if they shout and yell at their colleagues or competitors, it is because liberty of speech is to them a reality and not a form. The excitement of their streets is a purely intellectual excitement. They are trained eternally for street fights, and their very traffic is a street fight.

London has in comparison the ease and obscurity of a forest-glade. I do not know how far men still remember the very real genius of James Hogg, the Ettrick Shepherd, but he wrote at least one line which has the elements of eternal poetry. In the well-known song, "When the kye come hame" he describes the perfect conditions of love-making:

But beneath the spreading birk in a dell without a name.

It would be going too far to say that Addison Road was a dell without a name, but at least it has a name that nobody need pay any attention to. The London literary man may wander up Addison Road without any particular danger of his style (his rugged, suggestive style) becoming in any way Addisonian. A London literary man might with cheerful unconsciousness compose a Cavalier lyric in the Cromwell Road.

London, literally because it is chaotic and ill-governed, has for the literary man something of the careless contentment of nature. And, however much we may shatter abuses and reshape civic rights, it is to be hoped that this casual, erratic, and even secret quality will never be altogether removed from London ; for it is as essential to London as the sea to Venice. Nowhere certainly is it better expressed than in the peculiar quality of the literary part of London : in the smell and the spirit of Fleet Street.

A personal parallel will put the fact with a final clearness. In the great eighteenth century, almost contemporaneously, France and England produced two great men of letters. Each typified his country ; each ruled his time ; each was regarded by almost all men as an oracle ; each was, perhaps, the real ruler of his country's destinies through the after-centuries of revolution and war. In the blaze of the Paris sun, along the side of the splendid river runs the Quai Voltaire, with its great statue which almost defies the Cathedral. But if you know very well the dark and dirty byways of Fleet Street, if you love them for themselves, and search them patiently, you may at last find Johnson's Court.

ROMANTIC LOVE

THIS morning I read an article in a very serious magazine, in which the writer quoted the remark of Byron that a certain sort of romantic love is woman's whole existence. The writer then said that the first people who ever challenged this view were the revolutionary Suffragettes at the end of the nineteenth century. The truth is that the first people who ever maintained this view were the revolutionary Romantics at the beginning of the nineteenth century. The habit of giving to romantic love this extravagant and exclusive importance in human life, was itself an entirely modern and revolutionary thing, and dates from the romantic movement commonly traced to Rousseau ; but I think much more truly to be traced to the influence of the German sentimentalists. Most people who curse Rousseau have never read Rousseau ; or have only read the *Confessions* and not the *Contrat Social.* The critics read the *Confessions*, if only to condemn them ; because the critics themselves are modern romantics and sentimentalists ; men who like Confessions and dislike Contracts. The critics hate or avoid the *Contrat Social* not because it is sloppy and sentimental (for it is not) but because it is hard and clear and lucid and logical. Rousseau had his emotional weaknesses as an individual, like other individuals ; but he was not an eighteenth-century philosopher for nothing. What the moderns dislike about him is not the silliness of his confessions, but the solidity of his convictions ; and the fact that, like the old theologians, he could hold general ideas in a hard and fast fashion. When it comes to defining his fundamentals, Rousseau is as definite as Calvin. They were both ruthless theorists from Geneva; though one preached the theory of pessimism and the other the theory of optimism. I am not maintaining that I agree with either; but Rousseau would be as useful as Calvin in teaching some of his critics how to criticise.

But Rousseau is a parenthesis. Wherever the real Romantic Movement came from, whether from the German forests or the Geneva lake, it was a recent and revolutionary business, as compared with history as a whole. But it is obvious that the ordinary modern critic is entirely ignorant of history as a whole. He knows that his mother read Tennyson and his grandmother read Byron. Beyond that he can imagine nothing whatever; he supposes that his great-great-grandmothers and their great-great-great-grandmothers had gone on reading Byron from the beginning of the world. He imagines that Byron, who was a disinherited and disreputable rebel to the last, has been an established and conventional authority from the first. He therefore supposes that all women, in all ages, would have accepted the prehistoric Byronic commandment that the Byronic sort of romantic passion was the sole concern of their lives. Yet it is certain that women have had a great many other concerns and have been attached to a great many other convictions. They have been priestesses, prophetesses, empresses, queens, abbesses, mothers, great housewives, great letter-writers, lunatics founding sects, blue-stockings keeping salons, and all sorts of things. If you had said to Deborah the mother in Israel, or Hypatia the Platonist of Alexandria, or Catherine of Siena, or Joan of Arc, or Isabella of Spain, or Maria Theresa of Austria, or even to Hannah More or Joanna Southcott, that Byronic love was "woman's whole existence", they would all have been very indignant and most of them flown into a towering passion. They would have asked in various ways whether there was no such thing as honour, no such thing as duty, no such thing as glory, no such thing as great studies or great enterprises, no such thing as normal functions and necessary labours; incidentally, we may add, no such thing as babies. They differed a great deal in their type of vocation and even in their theory of virtue; but they all had some theory of virtue that went a little further than that. Up to a particular moment in the eighteenth century, practically every thinking person would have accepted the colossal common sense expressed by a French poet of the seventeenth century: "L'amour est un plaisir; l'honneur est un devoir".

Then came the extreme emphasis on romance among the Victorians; for the Victorians were not notable for their emphasis on virtue, but for their emphasis on romance. Queen Victoria lived so long, and the Victorian Age was such an unconscionably long time dying, that by the time Mr. Bernard Shaw and others began what they called a realistic revolt against romance, the sentimental German movement seemed to be not only as old as Victoria, but as old as Boadicea. It is highly typical, for instance, that Mr. Bernard Shaw, in one of his earliest criticisms, complained of the convention according to which anybody was supposed to have "penetrated into the Holy of Holies" so long as he was content to say that "Love is Enough". But, as a matter of fact, the very phrase "Love is Enough" did not come to him from any conventional or classical authority; not even from any conventional or conservative Victorian. It came from a book by a Socialist and Revolutionist like himself; from a book by William Morris.

Of course the anti-romantic movement led by Shaw, like the romantic movement led by Byron, has gone forward blindly and blundered in every sort of way. The modern world seems to have no notion of preserving different things side by side, of allowing its proper and proportionate place to each, of saving the whole varied heritage of culture. It has no notion except that of simplifying something by destroying nearly everything; whether it be Rousseau breaking up kingdoms in the name of reason; or Byron breaking up families in the name of romance; or Shaw breaking up romances in the name of frankness and the formula of Ibsen. I myself value very highly the great nineteenth-century illumination of romantic love; just as I value the great eighteenth-century ideal of right reason and human dignity, or the seventeenth-century intensity, or the sixteenth-century expansion, or the divine logic and dedicated valour of the Middle Ages. I do not see why any of these cultural conquests should be lost or despised; or why it is necessary for every fashion to wash away all that is best in every other. It may be possible that one good custom would corrupt the world; but I never could see why the second good custom should deny that the first good custom was good. As it is, those who have no notion except that of breaking away from romance, are being visibly punished by breaking away from reason. Every new realistic novel serves to show that realism, when entirely emptied of romance, becomes utterly unreal. For romance was only the name given to a love of life which was something much larger than a life of love, in the Byronic or sentimental sense. And anything from which it has passed is instantly corrupt and crawling with the worms of death.

HISTORICAL NOVELS

THE rapid change of literary fashions, which may be accountable for the temporary obscuration and the present resurrection of Anthony Trollope, is strongly marked in the current taste for fiction. There are fashions in novels as much as in bonnets or sleeves, though the great masters are little affected by them. A very thoughtful and widely read French critic, M. Emile Faguet, endeavoured to show that the "boom" in historical novels, which has been almost as obvious in France as it is in this country and in the United States, corresponded to a necessity of the human mind. He declared that the favourite types of novels varied in successive periods, and that it was now time for the historical type to enter on another period of vigorous life similar to that which it enjoyed in the first half of the nineteenth century under the genial and commanding influence of Scott. We have no Scott, worse luck—even Robert Louis Stevenson was "a very twopenny pirate", as his own Attwater might say—but we still read and re-read the Waverley Novels, and their spirit has again moved on the face of the waters of fiction. M. Faguet points out that realism, by its very nature and essence, is doomed periodically to weary its readers. The subject afforded by "contemporary manners", which alone the realist permits himself to paint, is necessarily limited. One La Bruyère is sufficent for a generation, and in the same proportion ten brilliant and two hundred respectable novels ought to be ample to cover the same time.

It has often been debated whether the historical novel is or is not a quite modern invention. In one sense there is no doubt about it; the first really great historical novelist was Scott, and his supremacy was so easy and so brilliant that many are content to count him the inventor of the type. The historical novel, in the modern sense of the word, was born about the time when the Ballantynes began—happily for us—to be pressed for money, and their poetical sleeping partner thought that it might be worth while to turn his attention to prose. Its second birth was in 1830, and the godfathers were Victor Hugo and Alexandre Dumas. At the same time, the careful student of literary genealogies can trace a much longer—though not a more honourable—pedigree for the historical novel. Mr. George Saintsbury carried the pedigree back more than two thousand years—to the times of Xenophon. The *Cyropaedia* is, no doubt, as near an approach to the historical novel as classical antiquity can show: which such as have read through that ponderous and dull volume will admit to be rather hard on the ancients. If some learned German iconoclast would, indeed, only prove that Xenophon himself never existed, and that the *Retreat of the Ten Thousand* was an exercise in historical fiction by some late Alexandrian —Porphyry, for choice—we should readily admit that Scott had a worthy forerunner. It is rather a long step—even for a genealogist—from Xenophon to Scott, but we can only find a few medieval romances, Icelandic sagas, and "chansons de geste," with which to make even a show of stepping-stones. One reason for this spacious void, of course, may be found in the very vague line which was, until quite recent days, drawn between history and fiction. It is only when the two things are kept carefully distinct that the "tertium quid" called a historical novel, which is really an artful blend of the two, can have any justification for existing. It seems to have been the sceptical and prosaic eighteenth century which first attempted seriously to define such a boundary. It has thus been said that we owe, in some sort, Scott and Dumas, *Salammbô* and *A Gentleman of France*, and *The White Company* and *Brakespear*, to Gibbon and Voltaire.

Before systematic historical criticism came into existence, all-armed like Pallas from the brain of Jove, it was hardly possible to draw a distinction between history proper and the historical novel. Pliny declared that all the world's historians down to his own time were but "narrators of fables", and his opinion still finds supporters, who unkindly refuse to acquiesce in his own exception of himself. Have we not seen Lord Wolseley enter Macaulay's *History* among the works of fiction which he was accustomed to carry for light reading on campaigns? "Whatever you read to me," said Sir Robert Walpole, "it shall not be history, for I know that to be false." Charles Kingsley was apparently dominated by the same spirit when he resigned his Oxford Chair on the ground that history was "largely a lie". Two, at least, of his successors, Freeman and Froude, would probably have expressed a similar opinion of one another's works. It has even been put forward, and seems to be a defensible if not a true opinion, that the whole works of Tacitus are a bold forgery of the Renaissance, in which case we should see our best authority on the reigns of Tiberius and Nero relegated to the shelf of *Quo Vadis?* and *Salammbô*. In the Middle Ages history and fiction had a persistent trick of merging into one another. "You never," said Mr. Saintsbury, "(or, at any rate, very seldom) can put your finger on any part of any medieval history, in prose or verse, whether it be avowedly chronicle or half-avowedly fiction, and say, 'Here the man consciously and deliberately left his facts and took to his fiction'." As long as this was the case, there could be no room for the historical novelist by profession; his place was usurped by the historian.

When, however, a new conception of the responsibilities of history slowly arose, and what is called " respect for the documents " began to sit on the pen and hamper the imagination of the historian, there speedily arose the demand for a previously unworked form of literature. A new maxim was constructed, which declared—unlike its predecessor—that, while the poet need not be a historian, the historian must carefully guard himself against Mr. Silas Wegg's tendency to drop into poetry—even as a friend. Even if he flattered himself that he had the true poetic heart, he lived in fear of the new criticism, and no longer ventured to adorn his historical works with the airy produce of imagination. It was no longer permissible for a Thucydides to ornament his work with speeches which might, would, should, or could have been—but never were—delivered, nor was there any longer tolerance for an Abbé Vertot to explain that " his siege was finished " when long delayed documents intended to explain that military operation arrived in due course of post. Sometimes the historian was driven to resort to Mr. Dick's expedient with his law-copying and his petition; he kept a work of fiction on the stocks beside his history, and turned to it when the afflatus of imagination carried him away from the dull and plodding work of investigation and reconstruction. William Godwin tried such a plan, and came very near writing our earliest historical novel in consequence. In his famous essay on Hallam, Macaulay ascribes a similar device to a well-known French historian. But the actual invention—and, for that matter, the perfection—of the historical novel in English was left to Scott, already a considerable antiquary as well as a poet, who might in other conditions or in an earlier age have become a reputable historian instead of the first of historical, and, perhaps, the greatest of all novelists.

ON WRITING BADLY

MANY people have suggested that every book ought to be reviewed as if it were published for the first time, even if it be Æsop's *Fables* or the *Odyssey*. In the first case we ought to say: "In the character of the Wolf Mr. Æsop has hardly broken fresh ground in moral psychology; nevertheless there is a certain quiet humour in this little work which is refreshing in these complex and morbid days." Or in the case of the epic poem we are to be imagined as saying: "By this work Mr. Homer has hardly added to his reputation. The success which attended his brisk and suggestive *Iliad* should not have betrayed him into supposing that the public would endure from him the mere garrulity of a ballad-monger." This idea is attractive, but after all it is unfair. In order to judge a book fairly we must not merely look at it as if we had never seen it. We must also look at it as if we had never seen any of its effects, of its branching influence, of its million imitators, of its eulogists, of its critics, of the eulogists of its eulogists and the critics of its critics. As it is we approach a masterpiece like *Hamlet* through the haze of an atmosphere which the masterpiece has itself created. We know that the thing is great before we begin to ask if it is good. There is something absurd in the very attempt to discuss how the thing should have been done; just as there is something absurd in the modern philosophical attempts to point out how the cosmos or the creation should have been conducted. How can we discuss how we should have written Shakespeare? Shakespeare has written us. And you and I (I am sure you agree) are two of his best characters.

In a very inferior degree, but still in the same significance, we may say that Alexandre Dumas occupies this primary position, from which he cannot be dislodged. He has many qualities in common with the classics, even with the classics who are much more important in literature than he. This certainly he has in common with the very great men : that he is indefensible. He sprawls at full length like Shakespeare, and shows all his imbecilities ; he is so open to attack that the word for him is not so much indefensible as defenceless, smilingly and superbly defenceless. He has the nakedness of the giants. He has that absolutely healthy characteristic of the really strong ; I mean that his weakness is mere weakness, and nothing else. His lapses are long, steady, healthy lapses, like great stretches of healthy slumber ; the strong man's stupidity is as strong as sleep. It is not, like the stupidity of lesser minds, merely a nervous nap. The man who wrote *The Three Musketeers* must certainly have been a man of startling literary talent and also of what the moderns call temperament, which means a power of seeing the world as the highly poetical thing that it quite obviously is. Yet this same man could write (or, as some say, cause to be written) hundreds of novels of which *Ascanio* and *The War of the Women* are examples : colossal and interminable volumes in which there is often no trace at all of that sudden and swaggering inspiration which sent out D'Artagnan to fight three fire-eaters who were all each other's seconds, or which carried off a great English soldier and politician inside a wooden box. Writing badly anyone can understand who writes at all ; I for one do it perpetually. Writing badly is the definition of journalism; writing badly is almost in such cases the definition of living honestly. But writing badly on such an enormous scale ; writing badly with such immense ambition of design ; writing badly with such immense industry of words and pages; and writing so badly as Dumas did—these things are the marks of no common mind. It requires a great man to write so badly as that. It is as courageous as building an ugly Cathedral, and staring at it as it sits triumphant in the sky. It is as bold as building the great wall of China, and deliberately building it wrong. If Dumas was futile it was almost in the same sense that Napoleon was futile.

Good, bad, and indifferent, Dumas must be treated as a classic; good, bad, and indifferent, he must be published entire by those who care for classics. This course has been most wisely adopted in regard to all the works of all the great but uneven workers. Critics included among Shakespeare's works almost reluctantly such works as *Troilus and Cressida* or *Cymbeline*, merely with the result that another generation of critics said they were the only good plays of Shakespeare. The old and hearty admirers of Dickens were sorry that the uproarious Master of the Revels who had made *Pickwick* became at last so sad and faint and ineffectual as to descend to *Little Dorrit*. Whereupon Mr. George Gissing, a man of real literary inspiration, almost said he thought *Little Dorrit* was Dickens's best book. It is never safe to throw away the works of the best men as refuse; if you do you will have all the best critics with their heads in the dustbin. Nevertheless, we may all quite fearlessly assert the badness of great masses of their work, so long as we do not propose thus coercively to carry it into effect. Shakespeare and Dickens resemble Dumas, not only in the fact that their bad parts are very bad, but in the fact that their bad parts are very long. When they began talking nonsense they went at it steadily, and there was no doubt about it. You could compile, I should think, the worst book in the world entirely out of selecting passages from the best writers in the world.

Nothing shows more clearly the essential health of human

democracy in the judging of such things than the fact that it is just this unpardonable prodigality and prolixity that is most easily pardoned. In the abstract, one would have thought that it was safer to write no book than to write a bad book. In the abstract, one would have thought that if the public had damned anybody, it would have been the man who went on writing books when they wanted him to leave off. But as a fact, the mass of men has done for its favourite authors, like Dumas, exactly what one would have thought would have been most tiresome and impossible ; they have selected for themselves. They read the *Three Musketeers* with a just and honourable rapture. They read *The Memoirs of a Physician* with a definite pleasure. And they read *Ascanio* without any apparent resentment.

A SHY BIRD

I

THE problem of presenting the English culture to that general European culture, of which it must always be a part, is made more problematical by one practical fact; which is partly an accident. It is the coincidence that the very best English things have to be translated. And anybody who has ever tried to translate anything knows there is continual danger of a sort of despair; he is tempted to say that what has to be translated is always what cannot be translated. From the standpoint of anyone who can see it from the inside, but see it sanely, the best things in England are poetry and humour; and it so happens that they are both locked up in a language. The Continent can be more cosmopolitan, partly because Continental countries have produced masterpieces in more cosmopolitan arts. You do not need an Italian dictionary or a Spanish phrase-book in order to appreciate a statue of Donatello or a painting of Velasquez. And the other two great cultures of Western Europe both in some sense escape from language, though they escape, so to speak, at opposite ends or at opposite extremes; one at the extreme of reason and the other at the extreme of emotion. France has affected and altered all nations by a logic almost as abstract as mathematics; and Germany has moved all nations by the wordless might of music. Now scientific argument can be translated; and music does not need to be translated. But some slight acquaintance with the tongue talked in one particular corner of the Continent of Europe is necessary in order to realise that " night's candles are burnt out " is rather fine poetry, or that Mr. Swiveller's gazelle who married a market-gardener is distinctly funny.

But this has a sort of secondary result, even in contacts necessarily cosmopolitan or international. We also, of course, must have a diplomatic language; but we have never had the knack of putting much of what is national into what is official. It is a paradox; or it would seem to the more logical nations a paradox, for it means that there is less of what is national in what is said in the name of the nation. It is a paradox to say that what is responsible is not representative. But the English are the most paradoxical of all the peoples of the earth. And whatever be the reason, it is certainly the fact that the organs of the State are very seldom the really organic organs of the people. Of all peoples we English are possibly the most purely patriotic, possibly excessively and narrowly patriotic, but anyhow tacitly taking the nation as a sort of religion or substitute for religion. And yet we have hardly a decent patriotic song to our name, and nothing whatever in the way of a National Anthem or official patriotic song that any of the singing or marching nations would tolerate for ten lines. If any intelligent foreigner would get a glimpse of the paradox that is the secret of the English, let him compare the astonishingly low literary level of the patriotic music-hall song, about waving the flag, with the exceedingly high literary level of the domestic music-hall song, about hanging out the washing. As has been said, poetry and humour are the good fairies of England; and the poetry may be found in the poor man's front-garden and the humour in the poor man's backyard. By another quaint perversity we alone retain a Poet Laureate, when we have lost touch with those ancient classical or medieval traditions which would make much more comprehensible to the Continent the idea of an official ode or a national bard or a minstrel singing before the king. One or two of our best poets have been Laureates, and one or two of their very worst poems have been Laureate Odes. But our very best poet came from nowhere, and very much resembles our very greatest humorist; for in that sense both Shakespeare and Dickens were poets, and poets coming from nowhere and even going nowhere. Neither of them can be quite conceived as going into the Government service and becoming the official voice of the English State. They lacked something of that classic solidity which can alone give dignity to a completely collective institution like the French Academy or even the Comédie Française. Even when talents of that classical type exist among us, they exist under conditions that are so individualistic or patchy or sectarian that it is difficult to use them as they were used in the great classical century in France by a classic dramatist who could command a chorus. We have had perhaps two poets, of very different scale, who had by nature that sort of impersonal grandeur that might have given dignity, as did the French classic poets, to an accepted loyalty to a great monarchy. And Landor was a Radical and Milton was a regicide.

Now it cannot be denied that in many merely international relations we have to remove an impression of pomposity. But pomposity is only the failure of pomp. So we say that an actor is too theatrical, because he is not sufficiently at home in the theatre to be dramatic. We fail in official poetry, or official prose, or official proclamations, because it is not our job and we do not do it well. But we fail in common intelligence if we do not realise that other nations often do do it well. We must not underrate the achievement of France in making drama a public institution, or of Germany in making music a public institution, merely because we ourselves are not very bright about institutions. We must not make a superiority out of an incapacity; but we must, and the increasing international pressure forces us to repeat most emphatically that we must, make other nations understand the nature of our capacity and the things of which we are really capable.

We all recognise the curse on those who say that charity begins at home; that they so often mean that charity ends at home. But by various historical accidents it is unfortunately true that English charity has had no obvious duty except to begin and end at home, not because England would not have sympathised with Europe, but because England knew hardly anything about anything but England. This fact has unfortunately hidden the much more important fact that English charity is really quite exceptionally charitable. When seen from the inside the English are of all the peoples the most soft-hearted; I shall not deny that it sometimes bears a resemblance to being soft-headed. On the other hand there is an international impression at least a hundred years old that the Englishman is cold and proud and insensitive. The problem of explaining the English culture is the problem of explaining these two things together and inducing the foreigner to look at the inside rather than the outside. In other words, in some way or other he must come and find us at home, not necessarily by coming to our country, but by reading the books or knowing the circumstances in which we are most at home. It is exactly the humanity of England that has never been explained to humanity.

Now it is exactly here that a sort of rescue comes with a real experience of some of the finest foreign culture. For it is not only the finest but even the most fastidious foreign critic who can sometimes appreciate our coarsest or most comic creations. He can often appreciate what we do not appreciate;

because it is too popular to be fashionable. I live in dread that some European judge will discover the vigour of our Cockney Comic Songs ; and publish them, as we should have done, in a companion volume to the *Golden Treasury*. Anyhow, it is a very practical clue to the right method in the matter. We might well suppose, for instance, that of all thinkable things Pickwick would be most essentially and exclusively a sort of family joke. But large numbers of Frenchmen know it is a good joke. Any number of Frenchmen would have seen the fun of the jokes of Pickwick who would have seen nothing but the cant of the speeches of Pitt. Daudet almost modelled himself on Dickens ; Maurois might be called a Dickensian ; and there is a real imprint of Dickens on French literature, precisely because it is the imprint of entirely genuine English literature. It is interesting to note in international influence the difference between Dickens and Thackeray. Thackeray, with all his merits, was only too much the English gentleman who represents us abroad. But Dickens really works for us abroad, precisely because Dickens was only at home when he was at home. Thackeray, Anglo-Indian by birth and Anglo-European by travel, never quite understood Europe, just as the Anglo-Indian never quite understood India. Dickens never tried to understand either of them ; but the result is that Europeans who love sincerity do want to understand Dickens.

Now the Englishman at home is almost the exact opposite of the Englishman abroad, or at least the legend of the Englishman abroad. Daudet, whom I have mentioned as an admirer of Dickens, expressed surprise when he visited England to find the people so different from what he had expected. For he had expected " men with all the vices of conquerors". Of course the English, being weak and human like other people, love to be told that they have the vices of conquerors.

Indeed, I almost feel a sort of traitor to my country in giving them away by saying that they very often have the virtues of saints. Especially the patience of saints. But if anybody wants to understand that patience he will find it much more genuine in Pickwick than in any Pacifist pamphlets. Note how Dickens takes for granted the patience of old Weller with his preposterous wife and her preposterous pastor, whom he nevertheless shows himself capable afterwards of ducking in a horse-trough, and you will be very near the nerve of something that is really English. The question is, how can we explain so secret a virtue to those who have other virtues, and cannot directly perceive that we have this one? Only one thing is certain; that we cannot do it by perpetually calling ourselves virtuous.

It is vital that we should avoid the appearance of offering ourselves as moral models, not because we have not moral advantages, in this or that respect, even as compared with others, but because we have not the intellectual advantages that would enable us to make the comparison or anyhow to make it correctly. In other words, our difficulty in helping them to know us has been, not only that we did not know them, but also that we did not know how much they knew already. There are some features about which some foreigners know much more about us than we do ourselves, but they are not the most genuine or the most general features. For instance, the fact that our populace does not really care much about politics, especially foreign politics, really acquits such a people of many charges that foreigners might bring, even if it might be a charge in itself. Our newspapers never tell us very much of what really is said about us, or against us, by responsible opinion; but the fact remains that the most genuine truth about England is to be found in England and not in what Europe says about England or England says about

Europe. The former may be a muddle or a misunderstanding, but there still remains something much more worthy of being understood; and concerning that we come back to what may seem the same somewhat frivolous moral, that it is much more likely to be found in our novels than in our newspapers.

II

Continental criticism, broadly speaking, has made a mistake about England. It was a very natural mistake, founded on certain superficial truths, such as those which have so long hidden from England the thrift and the tenacity of France. It largely arose out of the religious quarrel and the rise of the Puritans. And the Puritan was the sort of solitary figure which, when it happened to appear in one particular country, frequently falsified international impressions. Such a person is associated with such a place, not so much because he is often found there as because he is never found anywhere else. Nowhere else has the Puritan been dominant as he was in this island; for his presence here was despotic rather than democratic. His original power was due to militarism. His more modern power is due to plutocracy. But the English populace has never been Puritan even in the sense in which the Scottish populace has been Puritan; still less in the sense in which the Irish populace has been Catholic. Nobody who thinks in terms of real popularity, right or wrong, can have the smallest doubt about whether our democracy is normally on the march to Exeter Hall or to the Derby.

Along with this historical accident of the Puritan aristocracy went several other things equally accidental. A certain shyness and moody embarrassment that come from much more complex causes; the fact that, like most Northern peoples, including the Northern French, we have not the rapid gestures of the South ; an exaggerated reputation for roughness, curiously compounded of the legend of physical exercise and the legend that business is business, combined, with the puzzle of Protestantism, to create on the Continent an imaginary Englishman as stiff and stern as a Prussian. So far the mistake need not have troubled us very much. Nations normally do misunderstand each other ; and it is not worse than the notion that the Frenchman is immoral or that the Irishman does not know what he wants. Unfortunately, this slander had in it something horribly like a compliment. Still more unfortunately, some Englishmen were so weak as to accept the compliment. They liked to be called stiff because they thought it meant that they were strong. They liked to be called solemn because they thought it meant that they were responsible. Vanity of this sort is not of course peculiar to them ; it is common to the whole human race. But it was simply out of the weakness of vanity that they confessed to the sin of pride. In reality, they are not particularly proud and certainly not in the least stern ; they are an exceptionally kindly and even soft-hearted people. They do not even take their pleasures sadly ; they only take an incidental and I think regrettable pleasure in being called sad.

The meaning of Merry England was in this old original character of the English. In medieval times their public and proverbial character was festive and full of fun ; and even in modern times their private and personal character is the same. The witness to it is the great national literature, especially as it was when it was still entirely normal, and had not been crossed and confused by the self-conscious poses of more recent times. The last full and free manifestation of this normal and national spirit is represented by the name of Pickwick. It is the last expression of the complete freedom and fullness, not only in the literature of England, but even in the literature of Dickens.

The truth about the English adventure even outside England, is that the type of endurance has not been stoicism but rather tolerance. We might say it was much too tolerant, if it had not the rare virtue of tolerating the intolerable. What has really made the English, apart from mere jingo journalistic flatteries, a success in colonies and in campaigns in savage countries, was a certain comic acceptance of the incongruous ; a certain capacity in the English Cockney or yokel of continuing to be absurdly like himself even when, in the ritual formula, he don't know where he are. This is a national merit which, like other national merits, is gained at the expense of missing other things ; of missing, for instance, the full status of the citizen and the full inherited experience that comes of remaining rooted in very old civilizations. But it is perhaps the most humorous and attractive of all national virtues ; and men who really know from the inside the various nations of European humanity have found nothing more human than the ordinary English comic song or the talk of the Tommies in the trenches.

Nothing is more English than the fact that a band of comrades are comic in their incongruity. They differ and do not quarrel ; or they quarrel and do not part. There must have been many groups of Englishmen in camps and colonial holes and corners, consisting of men who got on with each other somehow, though each was regarded lightly enough as an individual. They were comic characters, if not to themselves, at least to each other.

The English spirit is really a shy bird, and differs therein from both the American and the German Eagle. And the shyness is mixed up with that misunderstanding by which a people very poetic have come to be called prosaic ; and the bird is indeed as shy as the nightingale in the dark wood of Keats or the albatross flying over the desolate seas of Coleridge. We must above all things be the reverse of vulgar, and therefore the reverse of vainglorious, if we are really to convey what freedom, what humour and what greatness of heart are hidden in the very seclusion of England.